A WRETCH LIKE ME
Victory Over Darkness

Clint Burwell

A Wretch Like Me

Copyright © 2022 by Clint F. Burwell. All rights reserved.

No part of this publication may be reproduced, stored in a retrieval system or transmitted in any way by any means, electronic, mechanical, photocopy, recording or otherwise without the prior permission of the author except as provided by USA copyright law.

The opinions expressed by the author are not necessarily those of URLink Print and Media.

1603 Capitol Ave., Suite 310 Cheyenne, Wyoming USA 82001
1-888-980-6523 | admin@urlinkpublishing.com

URLink Print and Media is committed to excellence in the publishing industry.

Book design copyright © 2022 by URLink Print and Media. All rights reserved.

Published in the United States of America

Library of Congress Control Number: 2022913573
ISBN 978-1-68486-235-1 (Paperback)
ISBN 978-1-68486-236-8 (Digital)

18.05.22

PREFACE

YOU HAVE PURPOSE! As God's people, no matter who you are, no matter what you have done, God loves you, and you have purpose. There was a time in my life when I thought I would never walk in what I believe God had called me to. But today I know that Jesus Christ is Lord. Today, it is my prayer that you too will come into your purpose. I sense the presence of God as I write this to you. Jesus is the lifter of your head. Some day you will understand that what you have gone through, and what you are going through right now, God will use to bring you into your purpose and glorify His name.

Allow Jesus to stand you up on the inside so people can see Him through you on the outside. It's your season. Look to Jesus now!

CHAPTER ONE

"CHOSEN BY GOD"

At the beginning, I too did not understand that the very thing Satan was trying to destroy me with, God would use to glorify His name and bring deliverance into so many other people's lives. I've learned not to be ashamed of my past. I've given my past to Jesus that He may use it, as it pleases Him. Through Jesus Christ you, yes you, have been made more than a conqueror through Him that loves you.

> *Who is there to condemn [us]? Will Christ Jesus (the Messiah), Who died, or rather Who was raised from the dead, Who is at the right hand of God actually pleading as He intercedes for us?- Who shall ever separate us from Christ's love? Shall suffering and affliction and tribulation? Or calamity and distress? Or persecution or hunger or destitution or peril or sword? Even as it is written, for thy sake we are put to death all the day long; we are regarded and counted as sheep for the slaughter. Yet amid all these*

> *things we are more than conquerors and gain a surpassing victory through Him who loved us.* Romans 8:34-37

Listen my friend, I made it through and so can you. You may be reading this book and don't know Jesus; well guess what? Jesus died for you, and He loves you.

I grew up in a Baptist home and church (in a small town in North Carolina) and even though I was taught to go to church, as well as "made" to go, I knew very little about God. I realize now that God had placed a desire in me to get to know Him, but as a young child I didn't understand.

As a child, my very first experience with God was when I had eaten too much and was afraid to tell my mother. Growing up, my grandmother and mother would tell me and my brothers and sisters: "You can eat all you want, but you better not come to me and tell me your stomach is hurting, because you should have sense enough to know when you are full." Well, that's true, but sometimes it's so good that it's hard to stop. Well, of course I didn't stop, and while lying on the floor in my bedroom, I started crying because I had eaten too much. As I cried, a very gentle voice spoke to me and asked me, did I believe he could stop the pain. I knew then it was God but had never really experienced this type of presence before.

Well, Jesus told me to put my hand on my stomach and ask Him to stop the pain. I did as He said, and right then my stomach stopped hurting. I can barely remember my age, but I believe I was around 11 or 12 years old. Jesus let me know right then that not only was He there, but He cares about everything that affects me. So, listen, it really doesn't matter how small or how great the problem may be, Jesus cares and He will step in to fix it. At that particular time, I had not been led to Jesus through the sinner's prayer. But I realized then and now, that no matter how distant Jesus may seem to be from you, even as someone that has never been led to Jesus by someone else, He knows your heart and He's closer than you think.

I thank God for my parents today because they took me to church. Even though they did not lead me to Christ through the sinner's prayer, they planted the seed. I remember what the Apostle Paul said.

> *I planted the seed, Apollos watered it, but God has been making it grow. So neither the one who plants nor the one who waters is anything, but only God who makes things grow. 1 Cor. 3:6-7 (Amp. Bible)*

Thank you, Mom and Dad for planting God's word in my heart.

As I said earlier, I was brought up in a traditional Baptist church. I experienced many things during that time that I will share with you in this book. At that time, I really did not understand and really didn't have anyone I could call on to explain what was going on in my life. As you read this book some of you may find yourself in that position and feel like you don't have anyone to go to. I understand because I was so afraid that people would stone me with words and not reach out to me with love. This led me into a very difficult life both spiritually and physically. But I tell you today; I have the victory. Beloved, you too have the victory that Jesus gave us through His shed blood and His resurrection.

As you read on, you may feel that your problems are not in this book. However, understand this. No matter what the problem may be, God is greater. He's able to change your circumstances and you can experience the power and presence of God in your life. He is standing ready, right now just where you are. Go to your knees, if you can, right now and ask Jesus into your heart as your Savior and Lord and He will come in and change your life.

As a child, I was never taught about the Baptism of the Holy Spirit. We had revivals and I remember as a young child, I went to the mourner's bench and joined the church and was baptized. But I had never accepted Jesus during that time. So literally, I was still on my way to hell. But you see; that's tradition.

For me, it seems like it all started at the age of 16. God came to me and said that He would fill me with His spirit. God had already given me the desire to preach His word, but I was about to experience encounters with God that many people, even preachers, would not believe. I was about to experience through dreams and visions the war between light and darkness, between life and death, and between love and hate.

It was at this time that God came to me in the form of a trance. I was not saved. However, I knew that God was changing my life and direction and I didn't know who to tell what I was going through. Like I said, I came from a traditional Baptist church that, I believe at that time, knew nothing about being filled with the Holy Spirit. I can remember the dream just like it was yesterday. It was a hot summer's day and after being outside for a long while, I went indoors to the kitchen. I got a cold glass of milk and went to my sister's room and sat down on the edge of her bed. I had just sat down when I fell into a trance.

Now falling into a trance was a pretty scary thing to tell at first, because I had nothing else to relate it to at the time but the devil. At that time, I had very little Word in me, if any Word at all. When I heard the word trance as a young teenager, the only thing that I could think of was witchcraft. I must tell the truth. All the friends I had as a 16-year-old were all in the world even if we all went to church together. Watching television shows that only lifted up the devil didn't help; and hearing other people talk, adults in particular, who didn't know the Savior made me feel like I was some strange, sick person who had done something to tap into a spirit world that I didn't know anything about. Anyway, I fell into a trance just like Peter did.

> *"But he became very hungry and wanted something to eat; and while the meal was being prepared a trance came over him."* – Acts. 10:10

Looking back at it now, I realize just how blind some people that go to church can be. There are many people today that still don't believe the Word of God. I'm amazed at how many people, still today, don't know that they can be filled with the Holy Spirit. In fact, what they need to know is that if they are going to do the work of Christ, they must be filled with the Holy Spirit. In order to be the witness that Jesus Christ speaks about in Acts, you need the Baptism of the Holy Spirit. But that's another topic.

While in the trance, I saw myself standing out in utter darkness. I turned and looked, and I saw a spirit in the form of a man running towards me, and just as it got to me, it leaped inside of me.

Now, just as that spirit leaped inside of me, another spirit leaped out from me and ran away from me as hard as it could. As all of this took place, I heard the voice of God say "I shall fill you with my spirit," and a cool breeze blew from my feet all the way up my body. It felt as if it was going to take my breath. I realize now that the breeze I felt was the breath of God.

And when he had said this, he breathed on them, and said unto them, receive ye the Holy Spirit. - John 20:22

After God had told me He would fill me with His spirit, I set up and found myself sitting on the edge of my sister's bed in amazement. For the first time, after reading in Acts over and over again about the Holy Spirit, the Father had spoken to me. I want you to remember something, I had not confessed Christ as my Lord and savior but God knew my heart and He came to me.

After this event, it seemed like all hell broke loose. I became very interested in the spiritual world, but of course without the proper guidance, I lean toward the dark side of the spiritual world. I can remember telling my Dad about the trance and he looked at me and said, "you are the one". Well, I was thinking the one to do what?

As I said, I became very curious about the spirit world. Even though I was going to church. Satan was forcing his way into my life more and more, as God was revealing Himself. Many times, I would come home from church and read the bible. Particularly, I would read the book of Acts and would stop as I read the Acts of the Apostles. As I read, I would say out loud, "I don't see these things in my church."

Before I go on any further, let me say this. There are people out here that are supposed to be walking with God but will say that God doesn't do things like that anymore. Well, if I can't credit what had happened to me to God, who then but the devil can I give credit to? I can remember telling other Christians and even one Pastor some of the things that happened to me-that I will later share. He in so many words told me that God didn't do stuff like that and for God to do something like that He would have to stoop really low. At that time, I didn't know any better but, If I could see him today, I would ask him could God have stooped any lower when He became Jesus, in the form of man, and died for our sins? Now, I know what happened to me, but that Pastor really left me in the cold.

Listen, God spoke in dreams and visions then and He still speaks to man in dreams and visions today. The church is suffering because of a lack of truth. We must be willing to share what Jesus has done for us today and not be ashamed of our past. Our testimony of what Jesus Christ has done for us, as well as what He has revealed to us, and how He has made Himself known to us is vital to others who need their deliverance through Christ. That is why I must yield myself to the Holy Spirit and allow God to use my life to glorify His name. This is the season of empowerment by the living God, and we as the people of God must be willing and ready to obey the voice of God when he speaks.

Listen church, don't become self-righteous and lose your ability to be used by God. If it had not been for the Lord on your side (our side) where would you be? Stop throwing stones and start reaching out in love. Stop talking about what you don't know about and ask God to show it to you. I've met some people in the body of Christ that have (so they think and act) gotten smarter than God. There are many people that have been lead down a wrong path because of someone else. Listen just because it didn't happen to you, don't mean that God doesn't deal with others like that. There is something great that's about to take place and I want to be a part of it.

> *And these attesting signs will accompany those who believe: in My name they will drive out demons; they will speak in new languages; Mark 17:17 (Amp.)*

Well let me tell you something, I got filled with the Holy Ghost in a similar way as seen in Acts. When I got saved and filled with the baptism of the Holy Spirit, I was in Italy. After I had received Christ (a few weeks later) one Sunday after church, I was reading a book entitled, *"The Holy Spirit and You"*. As I was reading the book the Preacher that actually lead me to Christ asked me had I received the baptism of the Holy Spirit with the evidence of speaking in tongues as seen in Acts Chapter 2. Well of course I said no. Well, on this particular day, we had gone to one of the member's home to eat and have fellowship. While waiting, the Preacher asked the owner of the home could he use one of their upstairs bedrooms. They said "yes", and we went up.

We went into a small bedroom that had one window and it was closed. His wife was with us and she was standing at that window praying. He told me to kneel at the bed and pray and to ask God to fill me with the Holy Spirit. I did as he said, and then he told me to begin praising God. As I started praising God, the preacher came and stood over me and asked me if I knew what the highest praise was. I said no. He said start praising Him with the praise "Hallelujah" and say it with all your heart. As I praised God, the preacher stood over me and placed his hands on my shoulder and prayed, "God, I'm not letting him up until he is filled with the Holy Spirit."

I got in the flesh for a moment, and I asked God to hurry up because my knees were starting to hurt a little. As we praised God upstairs in that room, a gentle breeze blew from my right side and passed by me to the left side. As this happened, without even trying to, I spoke in tongues. As a matter of fact, I stopped when I felt the presence of the Holy Spirit and heard the language that came out of my mouth. The preacher then told me not to stop the Holy Spirit but let the language flow. As I did so, I spoke again in syllables that later became a part of my prayer time and language. So don't believe the devil's lie that God doesn't do that anymore. I received the baptism of the Holy Spirit with the evidence of speaking in tongues in 1984 and I have been using that in my prayer time and teachings ever since that time. God is real and He is pouring out His spirit today.

If you are experiencing dreams and visions from God, let's look at the word to set it in stone. You see, if I had someone who I could have talked with to let me know what was going on in my life spiritually, maybe I would have come into God's will for my life sooner.

Just before we get into the word about dreams and visions, let me say this. The devil also came to me in dreams. He showed me how he wanted to possess my whole body and life, which I will go into deeper later in the book. But for now, let's see what the Word has to say about dreams and visions from God.

> *For I am the Lord: <u>I do not change</u>; that is why you, O son of Jacob, are not consumed. -* Malachi 3:6

I understand that this particular verse is speaking of mercy. But mercy is a part of His character, and so, I believe that if He did not change in His character speaking of mercy, He didn't change anywhere else in His character as well.

> *Joseph the husband of Mary was about to put her way secretly because he thought that Mary had lost her virginity. And Joseph being a just man did not want to make Mary a public example, was going to do away with the relationship without someone knowing it,*

and the Lord appeared to him in a dream. - Matthew 1:20 (Amp.)

And it shall come to pass in the last days, God declares, that I will pour out of my Spirit upon all mankind, and your sons and your daughters shall prophesy [telling forth the divine counsels] and your young men shall see visions (divinely granted appearances), and your old men shall dream [divinely suggested] dreams. - Acts 2:17 (Amp.)

Now I don't know about you, but I believe we can take God's word for it. But listen; if you have people around you that are preaching against this, and you don't know the Word of God for yourself, you might believe anything but the Word.

I truly thank and praise God today because He has proven Himself to me through His word. I know that God does speak today, and that He still speaks through dreams and visions. The church must wake up and walk in the word of God. The devil, through many people, tried to stop God's plan for my life. Down through the years I have learned for myself that the devil can't stop God's plan. I'm here to tell you that you have purpose and what God has planned for your life, will come to pass when you follow His will. Jesus has given you the victory through His death, burial, and resurrection. The Lord will work His plan in your life if you will agree with Him. At one time,

I had no idea that God had a plan for me. And even though I had to go through, Jesus was faithful to me and brought me out. And He will bring you through to victory too.

Don't let the devil rob you. It's your season to believe God. Write down the vision and make it plain so that you can run with it and achieve what God wants to do through you. I don't care what you have done or what you're going through. God can still use you. I know because I've been there and done that. It's time for you to stand up and believe God.

In this book, I will share with you the hell that the devil took me through because I didn't know any better and I didn't know anyone who did. Listen, the devil wants to make you feel ashamed about your past. I understand that. Now is the time to share how Jesus came into your life, saved you, and changed your direction and destiny. It's time for you to get up and allow God to use your past to shame the devil and glorify the name of Jesus. I give God praise for what He delivered me from and now I can share the love of God with the world.

The Lord has come to me in many other dreams and visions some of which I'm walking in today. Wait for their manifestation. However, I believe God. When I say, I'll wait, I don't mean that I'm sitting somewhere waiting and doing nothing. No! I mean I'm working the plan that He has already revealed to me as I wait for the other plans to unfold.

He has a plan for you as well. So, give your life to Jesus Christ if you're not saved. Stop right now and accept Him as your savior and Lord.

> *Because if you acknowledge and confess with your lips that Jesus is Lord and, in your heart, believe (adhere to, trust in, and rely on the truth) that God raised Him from the dead, you will be saved. For with the heart a person believes (adheres to, trust in and relies on Christ) and so is justified (declared righteous, acceptable to God) and with the mouth he confesses (declares openly and speaks out freely his faith) and confirms his salvation. Romans 10:9-10 (Amp. Bible)*

Will you trust Him with your life today? Jesus Christ is truly wonderful!

You may have been raised in a home, where you were told that you would not become anything. You may have been called names as a child and even as an adult, and those names have left a negative image inside you. Listen, God can change that image. I went through all that and I will share all that with you in a later chapter. But today I'm beginning to walk in His perfect will for my life. Yes, you will face opposition. Some of that opposition may be, and for some of you will be, in your character. However, Jesus can heal the hurt, build His character in you, and bring you into

His very own image by the power of His word and presence of the Holy Spirit.

My friend, the devil wanted to take my life either by physical suicide or through the process of sinful destruction. But Jesus would not let him.

> *But he who commits sin (who practices evil-doing) is of the devil (takes his character from the evil one), for the devil has sinned (violated the divine law) from the beginning. The reason the Son of God was made manifest (visible) was to undo (destroy, loosen, and dissolve) the works the devil has done.* 1 John 3:8

Beloved, no matter what condition you may be in, no matter how dirty you may feel, Jesus is your righteousness. His blood was poured out that you and I may be washed clean from our sins. Get up! Your purpose and destiny are calling you. The devil doesn't have the power to stop you from calling on the name of Jesus Christ. Oh, I give Jesus Christ all the praise for changing my life and yours. You may be reading this and saying to yourself, I have not asked Jesus into my heart. I'm believing God right now that as you're reading this book, the power of the Holy Spirit is drawing you to Him and into your purpose.

You may have met people that have told you that you have committed so great a sin that God can't use you. Well listen, that's a lie. If God can't use you, then

God didn't forgive you. God through Jesus Christ has forgiven you. Look at and believe the Word of God.

> *Therefore, I tell you, every sin and blasphemy (every evil, abusive, injurious speaking or indignity against sacred things) can be forgiven men, but blasphemy against the (Holy) Spirit shall not and cannot be forgiven. Matt. 12:31 (Amp. Bible)*

Every sin means every sin, but one. You may have gone through a divorce or even killed someone; you can be forgiven if you ask for it. Listen, what did Jesus Himself say when they hung Him on the cross. He said "Father, forgive them, for they know not what they do." I don't believe Jesus would have said that if He knew they couldn't be forgiven. So don't worry about people. Some people try to be God, but they are not God. I don't know about you, but I'm glad they're not.

What about the woman at the well that had a dialogue with Jesus in John Chapter 4? Jesus didn't condemn the woman, but simply revealed who He was to her and she left her water pot and ran back to the city and told the men there, "come and meet a man that told me all about myself, is He not the Christ?"

I believe she went back to the men she had been with, none the less she found her freedom and purpose in Christ. Jesus used her life to glorify the Father. And today God is using my life to glorify the name of Jesus. All the hell I went through was not for nothing. Just like the woman at the well, I met Jesus at the well and drank from the well of water that Jesus had to offer me, and now in me is a well springing up into everlasting life.

As you continue to read on, I hope you come to the realization that God has a plan and purpose for you. Allow Jesus Christ to step into your heart and stop the destruction that Satan is working in your life. If you're saved but still bleeding on the inside from your past, allow Jesus to heal the hurt, stop the bleeding, and bring you into your purpose today. God can take your life today and give you an abundant life. Through your life, Jesus can be glorified. Ask Him into your life right now. He's waiting for you. Jesus changed my life. He set me free from many things. I was dirty one time and could not share what you will read about in this book, but if this book will give hope to someone who needs it, then I willingly take up my cross and follow Him. I'm happy now because Jesus not only set me free from Satan and sin, but He also set me in my purpose. I lift my hands to Jesus Christ with praise on my lips and in my heart.

In other chapters I will share with you the spiritual warfare that took place in my life and how light overcame darkness. If you're looking for your place in life as a Christian talk to Jesus and he will order your footsteps. I know that He will, He did it for me.

When I gave Christ my heart, and He placed me in a Bible teaching church, I grew. God revealed to me that He would deal with me spiritually as He dealt with His people Israel physically. What was He telling me? God was telling me that as I read about how He dealt with Israel physically, I would learn His character. There are many people that are dying from spiritual starvation. God loves you. Stop believing the devil's lies through the lips of unbelievers. I hope you can remember that I said, that before I even got saved or confessed Christ as my savior, He was coming to me. Some would have you think that God won't talk to a sinner. Yes, He will. How do you think He drew you into the kingdom?

In Genesis Chapter 12, God spoke to Abram, whose name later changed to Abraham. Oh Yes! God called Abraham out from among his people and set Abraham on a path that would not only change his life but also eventually change the paths, directions, and the hearts of mankind back to Him.

Now it's your turn, and mine, to answer the call of God and let Him change our lives and our paths so that many others can be changed and put on the right path back to Him. Trust God with your life. Let Him use your past to give you and so many others a future. Do it today. Do it now! Your destiny is waiting. Have the spirit of Caleb and Joshua. Believe God and step out at once and take the city. Take the Promise Land.

CHAPTER TWO

"TRADITIONS OF MEN CANNOT SAVE"

Since the beginning, when God made Adam and Eve, Satan has tried to frustrate God's plan for man. But no matter how hard the enemy has tried to hinder God's plan for man, he has failed.

The devil tried to undermine God's will for my life, and he failed. When I look back at my life, I can see how the devil has placed people and obstacles of all kinds in my path to hinder and even stop God's plan for my life. What you must understand is that only you can hinder God's plan by willfully rejecting Him.

Well, it seems like all hell broke loose after Jesus Christ came and spoke to me that day. Don't let this frighten you, but Satan began to manifest himself to me also. Satan began to visit me in my dreams. For about five years he came to me in my dreams so much to the point that I was afraid to go to bed. I was afraid to fall asleep. There were nights when I went to bed, and it felt like a bear jumped on me. I realize now it was a demon spirit and he tried to pin me down to the bed. I was afraid to tell anyone, even my parents, because Satan had convinced me that if I told anyone they would not believe me.

People listen, I grew up in a traditional Baptist church and went every Sunday until the time I left home and joined the military. So, when I say that the traditions of men cannot save, that's exactly what I mean. I'm a Pastor now, but it wasn't until I was 24 that I gave my heart to Christ. We had revivals, the traditional way, once a year. On one occasion I was told to go down to the "mourning bench." Wellbeing afraid not to go, I went. I was totally confused about what I was supposed to do once I got there. The doors of the church were open and I went up and later got baptized. Well during that whole process no one lead me to Christ. That's right, no one. We had Sunday school every Sunday, worship service on the first and third Sundays, and we were taught some Bible doctrines, but no one actually led me personally to Christ. What is even more important is living the life that you preach about. No, I'm not judging anyone but at that time, I don't think there were many people saved in that church when I was growing up. I know now, more than ever, that my parents and others there could not teach me any more than they knew themselves. The church that I grew up in did not teach anything on the Baptism of the Holy Spirit. Since I've become a born-again Christian, I've learned many things. One of these things is the devil doesn't care if you go to church; he just doesn't want you to be born again and filled with the Holy Ghost.

> *And I will ask the Father, and He will give you another Comforter (Counselor, helper, Intercessor, Advocate, Strengthener and Standby) that He may remain with you forever* – John 14:16.

In verse 17 of the same chapter, He is called the "Spirit of Truth". Look at all of the descriptions used that show you what the Holy Spirit is to you as a believer. Stop now and take some time to look up those descriptions of the Holy Spirit. Once you understand this, it will change your life. That's why the devil doesn't want you to be filled with the Holy Spirit. The devil doesn't care how much you work in the church as long as you don't get Holy Ghost filled.

Listen, I grew up going to church but never experienced the power of God until I gave Jesus Christ my heart and got Spirit-filled as a believer.

The devil starts early in our lives to steer us away from God. As a child, Satan began by using people to call me names. Names mean something and names are words that can make you something positive or negative. The old saying of sticks and stones may break my bones but names will never hurt me is not true.

> *The words of a [discreet and wise] man's mouth are like deep waters [plenteous and difficult to fathom}, and the fountain of skillful and godly Wisdom is like a gushing stream [sparkling, fresh, pure and life giving].* - Proverbs 18:4

Did you hear that? Words from a wise man are life giving. Well, if words from a wise man are life giving, then words from an unwise man are destructive.

> *Pleasant words are as a honeycomb, sweet to the mind and healing to the body-* Proverbs 16:24

Since this is the case, then unpleasant words are the opposite.

Growing up I can remember being told that my legs look like a girl's legs. Well, some may say that these words should not have affected me. But you must remember that every person is not the same. Name-calling does affect people. If the name-calling is positive, then the effects will be positive. However, if the words are negative then the effects of these words will have on the person will be negative. What you must understand is that words build visions (pictures) inside of you. So, if you hear something long enough you will begin to see yourself that way. That's why the word of God is so important. The word of God builds a godly image inside of you. In my case, the devil used words to turn my character toward him. If your character is bad, so is your future. Oh, there may be a lot of people with a bad character in the world that look like they are doing well. But remember this; eternal life or eternal damnation is also a part of your future.

I really started struggling with who I was supposed to be as a child - and the struggle continued into my teenage years. Parents, if you have little children and even teens, listen to them and don't call them anything outside of the word of God. Mold your children's life through the word of God.

Many times, I was called a fool, stupid, or was told I would never be anything. I grew up with a fear of never being anything inside of me. I can remember how I thought I was going to disappoint my dad in life because I thought I was gay as a child. I thought I would grow up and become a homosexual and it all came from name-calling. I was so afraid inside and I felt like I couldn't tell a soul. As you can see, I grew up with a bad image of myself locked deep inside of me. I wanted out but didn't know how.

At the age of eleven or twelve I was introduced to masturbation. Now remember, I was brought up in a "traditional" church. I'm not kicking people who love the traditional setting, but I only hope that you are receiving the word of God and are being taught to have a personal relationship with Jesus Christ.

When I started masturbating, and while it felt good to my flesh like all sin do, I was opening the door for demonic forces to come in and completely take control of my life. Believe it or not church people never told me that masturbation was not a good thing to do. As I masturbated, I began to use my imagination, which began to lead me to greater perversions in my mind. Listen, your soul is the battleground for God and the devil. Because I was not getting the word of God, as I should have, the devil at the time was winning. There is no victory against the devil without the word of God.

In the Book of Matthew, Chapter 4, the word of God tells us that Jesus was led into the wilderness by the Holy Spirit to be tempted (tested or tried) by the devil.

> *And when he had* gone *without food for forty days and forty nights and after fasting the tempter came and said, If you are the Son of God, command these stones to be made (loaves) of bread. Jesus replied and said, it has been written, Man shall not live and be upheld and sustained by bread alone, but by every word that comes forth from the mouth of God.* - Matthew 4:2-3

So it is, we cannot defeat the enemy without the word of God.

Needless to say, that by the time I was a teenager, I was masturbating four and five times a day. It had become a stronghold of the devil in my life. But today I am free because of Jesus. Today, the devil has no victory in my life. Jesus Christ is now Savior and Lord of my life. I will share the conversion of me becoming a Christian in a later chapter.

I mentioned in the beginning of this chapter that Satan had begun to manifest himself to me. It seemed to me that these manifestations had become stronger than from the start. Satan began to see the plan that God had for my life and wanted to stop it. As I began to pray more to God, Satan became more vicious in his attacks against me. As I stated earlier, I was afraid to go to sleep because he would come in my dreams every night and show me how he wanted to possess my life. I honestly thought I was going to lose my mind. But listen, when the hand of God is on your life the devil can't destroy you.

Listen to me, you don't have to be or become anything the devil has lied to you about. The Savior, Jesus Christ, can set you free. You don't have to be a lesbian, homosexual, or anything that is not according to the word of God. I want to expose that lying devil now. You may have just come out of a perverted relationship and are now living a life free of that perversion but still may be having a hard time. Let me encourage you to stay in the Word and in fellowship with strong believers in the body of Christ.

Jesus Christ has made you an overcomer and you have the victory. I didn't say you would get the victory. I said you have the victory.

> *Then said Jesus to those Jews which believed on Him, if you continue in my word, then are you my disciples indeed. And you shall know the truth and the truth shall make you free"* -
John 8:31-32

There is a lot of suffering that is being experienced by Christians simply because they don't know the truth and you can't know the truth except it be revealed to you by the Holy Spirit. People suffer because of a lack of knowledge. But I'm glad to say today that the devil has been defeated and you don't have to live without joy and peace.

I said earlier that I had started masturbating and in so doing I used my imagination. First of all, the devil didn't create or give us (mankind) the imagination. The devil can't create anything. The devil can only copy and pervert what God has created. So then, imagination came from God. We must use our imagination to build images of righteousness within us by the word of God so that we can do the work of Jesus Christ.

Satan began to use my imagination as a tool to take me into greater bondage. I allowed the devil to take me from one perversion to another through masturbation and my imagination. That's why it is so important as parents to know what your children are watching on T.V. and what type of music they are listening to. Ungodly things will build ungodly images in them, and they will act on what is being built inside of them. However, godly things such as God's word, godly T.V. shows and music will build godly images inside of them. Why? Because the image of God is being seen and produced inside of them and they will act on what is being built inside of them. Now you can understand why the tradition of men cannot save.

There are still today people who don't take their bibles to church, and the only time they or their children hear the word of God is on Sunday. Understand this, two hours on Sunday is not enough to change the hundreds of hours spent in building ungodly image inside of them. I know. I lived it up until I got saved.

While studying at Biblical Life College and Seminary, one of the classes I took was "The Dynamics of a Spirit -Filled Prayer Life". The book "Dialogue with God" written by Mark and Patti Vickler was the textbook in which we studied from and one of the chapters dealt with the imagination.

There are three projectors that can project into our imagination. The first one is the devil. The devil wants to get a hold on your imagination. Satan will take something that is simple as a molehill and keep adding or projecting his thoughts into it until it soon becomes a mountain. That is what he did to me. He was using worldly people and some so-called saved folk to build negative images inside of me to promote his character and plan for my life. But thanks be to God! He sent His son to die for me and for all mankind to destroy the works of the devil. Satan uses our God-given imagination to project his thoughts into us. When this happens, we have allowed the devil to pervert our inner vision. When we realize this, we must learn to cut him off. Jesus and His word are the only way to cut off the enemy.

The second one is the "self-projected" image. We can project things into our own imaginations--on the screen of our hearts. Yes, we can paint images into our own imagination. For example, I can think of a car I like. Then I can think of the color I want and add that to the image. I can then see myself driving off the car lot with it by adding to that projected image I have already formed. This can go on and on.

The third projector is the Holy Spirit. When we allow the Holy Spirit to take control of our screen, inner eye, or imagination, while we are in prayer or in the word of God, we can then see with our inner eye the image of righteousness that the Holy Spirit is building in us and what God desires for our lives.

> *For though we walk in the flesh, we do not war after the flesh" (For the weapons of our warfare are not carnal (not physical weapons of flesh and blood), but mighty through God to the pulling down of strong holds; Casting down imaginations, and every high thing that exalteth itself against the knowledge of God, and bringing into captivity every thought*

to the obedience of Christ. - 2 Corinthians 10:3-5

Allow me to explain. Paul said though we walk in the flesh and live in the flesh we do not fight according to the flesh. Our weapons are not carnal or physical. Our power is in the Name of Jesus Christ and the word of God. Those strongholds and high things Paul were referring to were probably when he was overlooking ancient Corinth where there was a hill that was about 1,857 feet high. On top of that hill stood a fortress. A fortress is a military stronghold or a strongly fortified town. Paul used this imagery as an illustration of the war he waged. The fortress, towers, and captives represent the arguments, thoughts, and plans that Paul was opposing.

So, it is with us. There are fortresses that have been built in us from our childhood and evil thoughts and ways that have become military strongholds for the devil in our mind. Only Jesus Christ can overthrow these strongholds and build in us that military stronghold of righteousness that makes us godly people. I thank God today that through His word a fortified imagery of righteousness is being built in my imagination and I can see where the Father is taking me and what He is making of me. You too can become the image and the likeness of God the Father once again through the Son. But the traditions of men won't do it.

You may have just given your life to Jesus Christ and may not be getting the spiritual nourishment you need to grow. Pray and ask the Father to show you where He wants you in the body of Christ so that the right image, as a believer in Christ Jesus, can be projected in you.

> *Therefore if any man (or woman) be in Christ, he (she) is a new creature; old things are passed away; behold all things are become new* – 2 Cor. 5:17

So, tell the devil he is a liar. You have been made free through your faith, your trusting and relying in Jesus Christ.

Needless to say, as a young teenager leaving home and going into a society governed by the devil, I was helpless and confused as many people still are today. No one knew the spiritual warfare I was trying to fight alone. As I said before, I was afraid to go to bed at night for fear something, that I know now was a demon, would jump on me. It got so bad before I left home that I had to rock myself to sleep at night. One night my mother caught me rocking and asked me what was wrong with me. Being afraid to tell her, I said I didn't know. She told my father, of course, and they took me to the doctor. Remember, this was when I was a young teenager. You will not believe this but get ready to laugh. The doctor gave me something for constipation. Well, go ahead and laugh because I'm laughing now. But at that time, it wasn't funny. Satan was coming to me in my dreams just about every night showing me how he wanted to possess my life. Now he had started showing me, in my dreams, how he wanted me to kill and cut up people. As I sit here and think about this, I realize that people who hate for whatever reason are only trapped by the lie the devil has projected through imagery. Satan has built a fortified city of his evil thoughts and character in them.

Since no one could tell what I was becoming just by looking at me, I could hide the other person behind tradition. Tradition blinds you and causes you to accept who you are as being alright. It blinds you from the reality of who Jesus Christ really is.

I didn't look like I had problems but by this time, I had some real problems. The tradition of men is a merciless killer dressed in religious rituals. Listen, it can only dress you for death. Faith in Christ is the only thing that can save you. Today I realize there were family curses passed down through my family that were only broken when I accepted Jesus Christ as my Lord and Savior. The Lord taught me how to break those generational curses that had been passed down and to break the cycle to prevent passing them to my children.

As I said, I was a messed up young man and the problems would only get worse before I would finally give my heart to Jesus Christ. Sitting here thinking and writing, I'm so glad that Jesus Christ changed my life. Being a young man at that time and having no one I thought I could talk to about what was happening to me, I felt like I was under a lot of pressure and was going to lose my mind.

For five long years I battled the devil in my dreams and the thoughts that had become a fortress in my mind. I was slowly losing my grip on who I thought I was. During this period, I was becoming more of who the devil wanted me to be. Let me share this with you while it is on my heart. Satan wants to raise in America a godless generation. Where there is no word of God there is no image of God. Where there is no image of God there is no hope and faith in God. Where there is no hope and faith in God, one can only embrace destruction. That is what America is leading to.

Fighting a losing battle, I reached out to the world and all it had to offer. I was trying to hold on to my identity. I didn't really understand fully that Satan was the god of this society. Satan controlled the very things I was reaching out to. I was under pressure, and I was a teenager. Teenagers today are under a lot of pressure and influence from the devil that we, as adults, have allowed Satan to use as instruments of destruction. In other words, it is the adults, for the most part, that have become stumbling blocks for the generation behind us.

As a young man I was encouraged to sin. Being told repeatedly that I had time to get right-go ahead and have fun in the world. I was told this by people who went to church-church folk! Why do I say church folk? Because real "born again" believers in Jesus Christ will not tell you it's alright to sin. Now, ask yourself this; how many people do you know that go to church and say that they are saved, and still sin and say it's alright? Again, that's why traditions of men and religion are a merciless killer in disguise. The word disguise means to alter the appearance or to conceal the identity. Being in tradition and religion you can look like a Christian but carry an altered or concealed identity. And if you are not born again from above by God through accepting Jesus Christ as your savior, others will accept that identity as being right.

Being anxious to prove something to myself and to be accepted among my peers and church folk, that were telling me that sin was okay, I decided to try sex outside the will of God and make the devil a lie. What I didn't know then was, only the word of God-the only truth that exists-can make the devil a liar. Satan is the author of tradition and religion. So, living in those things couldn't make Satan a liar. Today, I wish someone had told me the truth. Everyone I knew, including adults, were telling me I needed to have sex. So, I did. During a process of time, I got a young girl pregnant, and she had a baby. But six months later the baby died. That made matters even worse. Of course, having sex didn't change the imagery that Satan had planted in my mind of myself. Only the word of God could have done that. I was never taught in a traditional setting that God values virginity. So again, I was thinking that something was wrong with me and maybe I was gay. All this time I still felt like I had no one to really talk to.

If you are not going to a church that is Holy Spirit filled and Holy Spirit led, you need to either ask God to fill that Pastor and the church with the Holy Spirit or ask God to show you where He wants you to be.

My friend if you are under this kind of spiritual attack and you are not a believer-a born again Christian from above by God-then you need to stop right now and get your Bible; turn to Romans 10:9, 10 and verse 13 and accept the Lord Jesus Christ as your Savior. In doing so, you will break the power of Satan over your life.

> *But he who commits sin (who practices evil doing) is of the devil (takes his character from the evil one), for the devil has sinned (violated the divine law) from the beginning. The reason the Son of God was manifested (visible) was to undo (destroy, loosen and dissolve) the works the devil has done.* - 1 John 3:8

Jesus came to set us free from the power of the devil and today, right now, the devil has been defeated. But you must accept Jesus Christ to walk in that freedom.

What I'm telling you is; the tradition of men cannot save. There are a lot of powerless people today that go to church because the traditions of men make the word of God to have no effect.

> *Thus you are nullifying and making void and of no effect (the authority of) the word of God through your tradition, which you (in turn) hand on. And many things of this kind you are doing.* - Mark 7:13

The traditions of men have kept many people bound and some I really believe have died and gone to hell because of it.

Well, as time went on, I joined the military. I became a part of the 82nd Air Borne Division. It was then that the dreams from God and the devil intensified in my life. I was with the 505th when one night, while staying in the barracks, a demon spirit finally manifested himself to me. I had been having dreams and now a demon stood before me in the middle of the floor of the room I was living in. I was then stationed at Fort Bragg, North Carolina. Still at this time, I was not a Christian. Let me inject this before I go on any further. I have always had an interest in the supernatural. I realize now that God was drawing me to Himself. However, without the proper guidance and someone to talk to that had the experience in knowing the spiritual world, Satan can come in and mislead you. As I said previously, I thought that I was on my way to demon possession.

Now, a demon spirit had manifested himself and was standing on the floor in front of me. I was lying on the bed in my room and this demon, who did not look like a demon walked over to me. You must realize without the spiritual discernment of the Holy Spirit the devil is not recognized. This demon looked just like a regular person, but when he opened his mouth and spoke to me I knew he was the devil. He spoke with a horrifying growl in his voice. I was lying there absolutely helpless. I had no power against him. He waved his hand in my face and I could fill the wind from his hand. After he finally disappeared from the room, I jumped up and ran out of there having no idea and no place to really run to.

Parents listen; get in your child's business. Know what they are doing. I did. I wasn't the most popular person in my home, but I was faithful to God in my home concerning the spiritual rearing of my children. Parents you might not have a clue to the ways Satan introduces your children to witchcraft. Your children are craftily and artfully being exposed to things. Parents know your children and their business. While in the world I met people who either knew someone or they themselves practiced witchcraft in some form. I did not realized this then, but now I do. One of the first places I was introduced to a form of witchcraft was in my own home. There was a book out then called "Transcendental Meditation". This also involved the use of the imagination. In this practice you could supposedly get to the point where you could move objects with the mind. This stuff is of the devil. This was another tool the devil used to make me believe I could use it to help me find myself. This goes totally against what Jesus said.

> *Whoever finds his (lower) life will lose it (the higher life) and who so loses his (lower) life on my account will find it (the higher life)* – Matthew 10:39

I did not fully realize that I was opening the door to a deeper spiritual experience with him (the devil?).

Well after that experience I called my family and told them about it, and they came to Fort Bragg to see about me. After talking with them and other family members about the experience I went through, I realized they had no idea what to do either. After they left to go home, I was once again left alone and scared out of my wits.

The dreams continued. But now, not only was he showing me in dreams how he wanted to possess my life, but he also started giving me thoughts about sleeping with the same sex. Would you believe that there are many people who go to church, as well as those who don't, who have the same experiences but are afraid to tell anyone for fear of how they will be looked upon? Saints, we have the answer that the world needs. But if you don't share your experience in Christ and what He delivered you from, many people will never walk in what Jesus Christ gave His life for.

Church, we must wake up and rise up to the place whereby Christ has freed us and empowered us to set the captives free. People are dying out there and we have the answer. At one time I was ashamed to write this book, but Jesus kept me and brought me through so that one day my life would glorify God. So, I've been bought with a price. My life is no longer my own. Jesus can use my life to tell someone about His love and forgiveness. Jesus said if I be lifted up, I will draw all men unto me. So, church let's lift up the name of Jesus through our witness of what He has done for us and all men shall be drawn to God.

The Bible shows how Satan has tried to hinder God's plan for man here on earth for many years but has failed. There are people in the body of Christ that feel God can't use them because of what has happened to them. Well let me be the first to tell you that's a lie. God can and will use you if you will allow Him. It is God's desire to bless you and He will when you realize that you are forgiven, and God has a plan for your life. So, take that bold step of faith. God is waiting to manifest Himself to you. Don't miss your season. Act on His word. He's waiting for you.

CHAPTER THREE

MY LOST IDENTITY

Joining the military, for me, I guess was a way of escape or so I thought. No matter where I went the devil was right there to torment me. In the previous chapter I spoke about how the devil manifested himself in my room and me running after he left. When other people started hearing about what was happening, guys who had dealings with witchcraft in some form or another came out of the woodwork. Little did I know that the Lord was with me and had never left my side.

While at Fort Bragg, I met a friend whose name I will not mention. We remained friends throughout my whole military career. The devil was making his move and I was completely oblivious to it. This was all in his plan to destroy me. He does it with everyone. He starts with you as a little child. That's the way he destroys one generation after another, and if someone doesn't look to God, a generational curse and the devil's desires will be promoted from one generation to another.

As I said he starts at you as a child through people who are not saved or people who are still carnal in their spiritual walk. Yes, carnal Christians. He plants seeds of fear and unbelief and being born in sin or with a sin nature we naturally lean toward Satan. We're born spiritually separated from God and into spiritual slavery under the devil because of the fall.

Let me explain something about the beginning of man and the fall of man. First of all, Satan attacks anything that is made in the image of God. Man was created in the image and the likeness of God. Satan is out to pervert anything that God made like Himself. That's why at an early age the devil begins to introduce children to all kinds of perversion through the structure of the family. The Bible says that Satan is subtle. In other words, Satan is cunning. Cunning enough that by the time you recognize the danger, it's already upon you. This is the reason why we must teach our children early and teach them the truth. The truth must be passed down from generation to generation.

Adam was really the only man made in the image of God. God's image is perfect. After the fall of Adam, men are begotten in Adam's image. Adam's image was imperfect and depraved with the law of sin and death working in it.

> *This is the book of the generations of Adam. In the day that God created man, in the likeness of God made He him. Male and female created He*

> *them; and blessed them and called their name Adam, in the day when they were made. And Adam lived one hundred and thirty years, and begat a son in his own likeness, after his image, and called his name Seth.* – Genesis 5:1-3

The third verse states exactly what I just said. Notice that Adam now has a son that is not in the likeness and image of God, but in his own image-an image that's unlike God. God breathed into Adam a divine spark of life. But every man after the fall, through Adam, was born in darkness separated from God. Man after Adam came with the natural ability to walk against the will of God. That is also why in the previous chapter I said that tradition couldn't save. It is only through faith in Jesus Christ can anyone be saved.

After I left Fort Bragg, I went to California. By now the friend that I mentioned earlier was going home with me from time to time. We had become good friends.

Leaving home of course made the playing field for the devil even larger. At the age of 19, I was a mixed-up young man trying to battle the images of negativity in my mind all by myself. Understand, without Christ there is no hope. Arriving in California I felt like I had no one to trust but my friend and myself. Listen, Satan knows how to bring people and things into your life to encourage you to do his will. I had no idea that this young man that had become a friend to me was battling with almost the very same thing.

As time went on, I got more involved in alcohol and drugs. Alcohol and drugs are a major door opener for the devil. As I became more involved in drugs and alcohol the more real the images became to me. You see; it was words from the beginning that painted all these images of perversion in my mind. Words, good or bad, spoken to you as a child have a very strong influence on the direction you may take in life. Coming up as a child and before leaving home Satan had already turned me in a terrible direction. I was having problems with my identity and with knowing who I was supposed to be. Now Satan had started to suggest to me that the images I saw in me were me and I should accept who I was. People, you must believe that everything that comes out of the mouth of the devil is a lie. The word of God says this:

> *You are of your father, the devil, and it is your will to practice the lusts and gratify the desires (which are characteristic) of your father. He was a murderer from the beginning and does not stand in the truth, because there is no truth in him. When he speaks a falsehood, he speaks what is natural to him, for he is a liar (himself) and the father of lies and of all that is false.* - John 8:44

Let's look at this verse a little closer. What we practice in our everyday life reveals who we belong to. Jesus said to the Pharisees, of your father the devil and it was seen in their practice-their practice was a characteristic of the devil. Notice something else about the devil's life as a murderer. Satan_ is trying to kill you. He starts with us at a very young age, when we are very vulnerable. He teaches lies that will not only take your life but can take so many others with you. Just as truth can be presented in many forms so can lies. And since lies are made up of words, let's talk about words again.

Let's look at the book of Mark and see what Jesus said about words. In Mark, Jesus revealed the power of words when they take root in the heart.

> *Truly I tell you, whoever says to this mountain, be lifted up and thrown into the sea and does not doubt at all in his heart but believes that what he says will take place, it will be done for him.* - Mark 11:23

Once something gets into your heart and you believe it, you then begin to say it. What you say produces what you believe. That's why the devil doesn't want you getting in the word of God. Once the word of God takes root in your heart, the images of righteousness are being built inside of you. You will say what you see and what you see you will believe. That's what was going on inside of me. But at this time in my life, it was Satan painting images through the power of words. He had built a fortress of lies and wickedness in me. As a result, I began to follow the images and the imaginations of my heart. Listen, what you see inside of you-the images that have been planted and growing inside of you-you will eventually act on. Get in the word of God and allow God to build righteous images of who you are in Christ Jesus. Why? Because what you see is what you walk in.

Let me give you one more example of what was going on inside of me as well as every person on the planet, whether it is good or evil. In Matthew the Word says:

> *The eye is the lamp of the body. So, if your eye is sound, your entire body is sound, your entire body will be full of light."* - Matthew 6:22

Let's start with the eye. The eye deals with vision and judgment. The eyes and ears are the gates to the heart. As a child what you see and hear you receive and make judgments on what you understand them to be. After those thoughts of what your eyes and ears received are computed, they are then stored in your mind's memory bank. If those thoughts are not dealt with they will get into your heart. Once in the heart you believe. What you believe you say, and what you say you have. So, listen, if what you're receiving through your eyes and ears is righteous and good,

Jesus said the entire body is full of light. But if you are not full of light then:

> *But if your eye is unsound, your whole body will be full of darkness. If then the very light in you (your conscience) is darkened how dense is that darkness.* - Matthew 6:23

Here Jesus is talking about the conscience. The conscience, however, deals with images. If every image you see within you is wrong, then more than likely everything you say or do will be wrong. What you say and do are seeds that you plant in life's soil. These planted seeds grow and produce a harvest. Simply put, if all you plant is something wrong then what you will get is something wrong.

That's what happened in my life. I had good parents that taught me good things but a lot of things that were negative got planted in me as well. Unfortunately a lot of the bad stuff got watered with words that fortified the lies about who I was supposed to be.

Well because I didn't have the word of God in me like, I needed it to be, I leaned toward the lies the devil had told me. It was only God who saved me from the clutches of an evil taskmaster. But, before I would turn to God completely, Satan will have done his damage. However, the damage was not too great for God, through his Son Jesus, to heal.

During this time, the eye of my body was completely dark. I could only see the images of what the devil wanted me to be. As I'm writing this, I'm smiling because I know what God is able to do. Today, God has brought to pass the thing He had promised me when I was a teenager. I now live my life for Jesus Christ and to expose the enemy of our souls. And I know the battle is not over yet because Jesus still has to come and get us. But I know He will, and I know that the victory is won.

Now, with a friend in my life to make the devil's plan possible, he tried to move in for the kill. Before I go any further let me say this; I'm probably going to make some family members mad, and some friends look at me differently. But as I said, I live my life now for Christ and no other. I will be like the woman at the well who, after talking with Jesus realized that He was the Messiah, ran and told everyone about a man that told her everything about her life. Jesus can use me. So, here we go.

After making the rank of sergeant, I was in charge of quarters (where the soldiers who did not live off post were housed). Having an image that was built as a child by the devil hidden, it was now trying to come forth. One night a young man who was gay, approached me. He stood before me and told me that he liked me. This was the same person that I recalled had followed me to the gym one day.

I told that person to come up stairs with me to my room. Well, when we got there we stood looking at each other and I kissed him. At that very moment Satan's plan for my life had been put into action. I had now acted on the image that Satan had planted in me. Satan thought he had me completely. I know I was wrong for doing this, but I was a slave to Satan, and I realize now that I was being driven to destruction. Please hear me when I say this; if you are in a homosexual relationship, you are wrong. It is sin and will lead you straight to hell. Satan is a murderer, and he is trying to destroy your life. God never intended for two men or two women to sleep together. He never meant for the same sex to be married. Now as a Pastor, I have talked to people that Satan has either led them that way or they almost decided to go that way. What I'm learning is that a lot of people have fallen into that trap some kind of way.

Well after that night I never really saw him again, thank God. But the struggle was still there. The battle was going on within me. Very few people knew that I was nothing but a walking time bomb. Outwardly, I was trying to show the hard nose sergeant in the military yet inwardly I was very fragile. Well, as time went on, I would have two more encounters with the same sex. No encounter was ever with penetration. It was always oral and was what I let them do to me. I am not proud of any of this. But again, if it will help anyone and keep people out of hell then Jesus, you can use me. I never got close enough to my friend to have a sexual relationship with him. We came close but the Lord would only let me go but so far. God kept me. I can remember when I was discharged with an honorable discharge, my mother told me she had prayed for me many times. You know, mothers can sense things when fathers can't. She prayed to God and said, "Father bring my baby home." She said she told God, "I don't care how you bring him home, but just bring him home to me." I will cover more of this in a later chapter.

God had spoken something to me and He was going to bring it to pass. No matter how hard the devil tried to stop God's plan for my life, God's word prevailed over all. I made it through, as you will read later. But there was still more to come before I would finally walk in God's will for my life.

Again, as time went on the drinking and the drugs would only get worse. I was trying to drown out the voice of the enemy and what I thought I had to accept concerning my life's destiny. I was trying to fight the enemy physically. Understand this, you can't fight the enemy with physical weapons. You can't fight a spiritual enemy in the flesh.

> *In conclusion be strong in the lord (be empowered through your union with Him); (draw your strength from Him); (that strength which His boundless might provides); Put on God's whole armor (the armor of a heavy-armed soldier which God supplies), that you may be able successfully to stand up against (all) the strategies and the deceits of the devil.*

For we are not wrestling with flesh and blood (contending only with physical opponents); but against the despotisms, against the powers, against (the master spirits who are) the world rulers of this present darkness, against the spirit forces of wickedness in the heavenly (supernatural) sphere. Therefore put on God's complete armor, that you may be able to resist and stand your ground on the evil day (of danger) and having done all (the crisis demands) to stand (firmly in your place). Stand there (hold your ground) having tightened the belt of truth around your loins and having put on the breastplate of integrity and of moral rectitude and right standing with God; And having shod your feet in preparation (to face the enemy with the firm footed stability, the promptness and the readiness produced by the good news) of the Gospel of peace. Lift up over all the (covering) shield of saving faith, upon which you can quench all the flaming missiles of the wicked (one). And take the helmet of salvation and the sword that the spirit wields, which is the word of God. - Ephesians 6:10-17 (Amp.)

To fight the enemy, you must draw from God. It was only through Jesus Christ that I found victory. There is no other name except through the name of Jesus can anyone be saved. This is now the time that we must cry out to the lost for Jesus Christ. That's why I wrote this book. Jesus is real and very much alive.

I was trying to fight an enemy that I knew nothing about, but Satan knew me all too well. For years he had poured darkness into me that I could not overcome by myself. I was drowning in a sea of confusion and hatred. Before I would be freed from Satan's grip, I would become very bitter-so bitter that I hated myself and everyone else.

This is how I know we serve a faithful and loving savior. In all my rebellion, He still remained faithful to His word. He kept His promise that He had made to me as a teenager-the wonderful promise of filling me with His spirit. It is so wonderful to know who Jesus is and how He keeps His word.

While I was in California, the savior gave me a mighty touch one night. On the very night that He would touch me, I was trying to get high. I will never forget it as long as I live. Another friend of mine came to me and asked me if I wanted to get high with him. I said yes and I went with him to his barracks. He took out some beer and marijuana and we started smoking and drinking. The entire time of indulging ourselves, I could not get high. Either the drugs and beer were no good or God had other plans. But for some reason that night I could not get high. By now, I was very unhappy with myself and tired of living. I recall feeling as though I was in hell, but Jesus was there too.

> *If I ascend up into heaven, thou are there, if I make my bed in hell, behold, thou art there -*
> Psalms 139:8

I praise God today for His loving kindness because this was exactly how I felt. There was a tremendous battle for my life going on inside of me. I told the guy that gave me the drugs, thanks but it just wasn't working. No matter how hard you try to drown out your sin with drugs, alcohol, or other fleshly ways, there isn't but one answer for sin-the blood of Jesus Christ. You must repent of your sins (do a 180-degree turn), turn to God, confess your sins, and accept Jesus Christ as the savior and Lord of your life.

I left his room and decided to run. I was a good runner then. I went to my room, changed clothes, and left out to receive an experience from God I will never forget. Fort Ord was based right on the coast of California and was right next to the water. I ran 5 miles that night-two and a half mile out and two and a half miles back. Feeling very confused, I ran to the coast, and I jumped the fence that was there around the post. I ran down to the shore and stood there watching the waves come in. I could feel the trembling under my feet as the tide came in. As I watched I was amazed at the power of God and was suddenly reminded of the creation of God and how He divided the waters from the land. I can remember thinking that God was so awesome in how He kept the water from coming any further than it did.

I started to walk when a voice in me said turn around and tell the devil to leave. I stopped and at first, I thought that was crazy, because no one was there. I surely didn't want to turn around and see Satan standing there. I had one encounter like that before. Realizing that it was God telling me to turn around and rebuke the devil, I turned to rebuke him. The moment I began to turn I could feel the presence of the wicked one. It felt like it made the hair on my neck stand up. I turned and obeyed God. I told the devil in Jesus' name; I command you to leave for I am spending time with my father. When I said that I felt the presence I had felt before suddenly leave. I turned about and again started looking out over the water. I then started talking to God about how I was brought up to believe that He actually existed, but now I really needed to know. I said that I was at the end of my rope, and I needed to know He was there. I started singing a very familiar song, "His eyes is on the sparrow, and I know He watches me." As I sang that song I dropped to my knees. I was now thinking of suicide. While down on my knees I heard again that voice, the voice of God, telling me to get up and finish my run.

Standing to my feet and starting back, I jumped back over the fence and started running as He had told me. I had been running only about a half-mile when looking up from watching my feet, to look up at the hill I was approaching, and I saw a pinkish glaze in the bushes that was at the right and crest of the hill. I slowed down trying to see what it could be. I was running on the sidewalk and remember there were streetlights but the glare I was drawn to was not coming from the streetlights. Having slowed down more I looked to see if I could go another way, but I couldn't. So, I kept my course but approached it a little slower. Just as I got to the peak of the hill where the pinkish glare was, I looked up and a red beam of light came out of the clear and starry sky and hit me right in my eyes. When this happened all the strength in my body left me and I found myself stretched out on the sidewalk. Not knowing exactly how I got there, with not even a scratch on me, I stood again to run and again I fell down to the ground. I never felt myself actually hitting the pavement. After lying there but just a moment, I set up and the pinkish glare that I saw in the brushes was now on me. It was something I had never felt before in my life and have never felt since. It felt so good I could taste it in my mouth. It was so sweet to the taste. I'm reminded of the words that David said about God in the book of Psalms:

> *O taste and see that the Lord (our God) is good! Blessed (happy, fortunate, to be envied) is the man who trusts and takes refuge in Him –*
> Psalms 34:8

I had never felt anything like that before. As a matter of fact, it was so good that I thought I was going to burst, and I screamed, "Lord have mercy."

The moment I said that; it lifted. I leaped to my feet crying and screaming: "God has touched me! God has touched me!" I really finished my run then! I don't even know who long it took me but when I got back to the barracks, I rushed through the doors with tears in my eyes and breathing hard. The guys that saw me ran to me and said, "Burwell, what's wrong? Did somebody jump you?" I said, "No, nobody jumped me". Then they said, "Well, what happened"? I said, "God touched. God touched me." They stood back and said "what"? "God touched you?" I said yes, He touched me, me! Well, by now they were thinking some of everything. Some said I believe you, because I never seen you this way. And other said, what have you took because I want some.

Needless to say, many of them did not believe me. I know now that some people out there today, including some Christians that will say they believe in God but won't believe me about my experience. However, that doesn't change what happened to me. The friend I told you about believed me. I can remember him taking me to a Pastor, on post. After telling him what I knew happened to me, he looked at me and said, "no doubt you had some type of experience, but I don't believe it was God." He said that God would not or could not stoop so low as to do that. Needless to say, I left confused from a person that I thought could give me some answers and guidance. However, I would not accept his answer. I couldn't find another person that could help me. I was left again with no one to help me. Reading from the Bible let's take a look at God's Word concerning Paul who had a road experience.

> *Now as he traveled on, he came near to Damascus, and suddenly a light from heaven flashed around him, And he fell to the ground. Then he heard a voice saying to him, Saul, Saul, why are you persecuting Me [harassing, troubling, and molesting Me]? And Saul said, Who are You, Lord? And He said, I am Jesus, Whom you are persecuting. [a]It is dangerous and it will turn out badly for you to keep kicking against the goad [to offer vain and perilous resistance]. Trembling and astonished he asked, Lord, what do You desire me to do? The Lord said to him, But arise and go into the city, and you will be told what you must do. Acts 9:3-6*

Now while I didn't talk to Jesus that night like Saul, I had what I called my Damascus road experience. I went to a preacher who basically told me I was lying and I know what happened to me. I wish I could see that preacher today and ask him do you think Jesus could have stooped any lower when He came in the earth as a man and took our punishment? Could Jesus have stooped any lower than in the 50th chapter of the book of Isaiah?

> *I gave my back to the smiters, and my cheeks to them that plucked off the hair: I hid not my face from shame and spitting. Isaiah 50:6*

For further references please read Matthew 26:67, 27:30 and John19:1. I sometimes wonder why that Pastor told me that. Even though I know there is racism country-wide in the churches of America, I don't like thinking that he said that because of my skin color. Unfortunately, in our society, racism exists in both so-called black and white churches. It makes me wonder if those people even read the bible. Just in case they haven't and so they will know, let's take a look at First John:

> *Beloved, let us love one another, for love is (springs) from God; and he who loves [his fellowmen] is begotten (born) of God and is coming [progressively] to know and understand God [to perceive and recognize and get a better and clearer knowledge of Him].*
>
> *He who does not love has not become acquainted with God [does not and never did know Him], for God is love.* 1John 4:7-8

I know what happed to me, and today I finally get to tell my story. I asked God how long it would be before I could tell what happened to me. Now, I know God wanted me to be able to tell the whole story because someone needs to know that God loves you. No matter what you have gone through God is still there for you. Jesus died for you and me and if you will turn to Him right now, He will abundantly pardon.

God is not pleased with any lifestyle that does not line up with His Word. But if you will repent of your sins and come to Jesus right now, He will forgive and cleanse you and fill you with the Holy Ghost.

Well, because I didn't have support (someone to tell me what I needed to do), yes, believe it or not, I went back to drinking and drugs. But don't get discouraged. There is more to this story, as you will see the glory of God as you continue to read. I had no spiritual guidance, and I went back to who I was hanging out with. I didn't' go back immediately, but because I didn't know how to stand, I eventually went back, and my condition got even worse than before. However, today I want you to know that I walk in complete victory. Yes, because of Jesus Christ, the devil didn't win. And he doesn't have to win with you. As a believer in Jesus Christ, if you are saved, Jesus has given you power over the enemy. If you are not saved, you too can have complete victory over the devil if you give your heart to Jesus Christ.

Before bringing this chapter to a close, I would like to leave you with this:

> *Beloved, let us love one another, for love is (springs) from God; and he who loves [his fellowmen] is begotten (born) of God and is*

> *coming [progressively] to know and understand God [to perceive and recognize and get a better and clearer knowledge of Him].* Luke 10:19

Stand up child of God and be in Christ what He has given you. Don't be afraid. Someone is waiting and needs what Christ has given you. If you are bound by sin you don't have to be. Jesus died so you can be free. Go to Him now, you're only a prayer away from freedom. Reach out! He's calling you.

CHAPTER FOUR

JESUS IS MY REDEEMER

Before leaving California, in my mind, I was locked in chains by the devil. Even after receiving warning after warning to separate myself from my friend that had been with me since Fort Bragg, I was reluctant to do so.

God had put a squad leader in my path, who was saved and filled with the Holy Spirit, to warn me and to let me know that God was calling me and that he could see the call on my life. Yet, because of a stronghold that had been planted in my mind by the devil when I was a child, it controlled my direction and desires.

Strongholds, I thought at one time meant devils flying around in the heavenlies. Yet while there are spiritual demons flying around controlling areas in our society, the strongholds that Paul referred to in Second Corinthians 10:5 are reasonings, theories, calculations, and deceptive fantasies or speculations in our minds. That's why the Word of God tells us in Romans 12:2 not to conform to this world or this age. Don't pattern your lives by the examples of this world. Listen, I don't like saying this, but not even by some people that go to Church. Why? Because there are people that go to Church that are not trying to pattern their lives after the life of Christ. It is very important that you get into the Word of God and study, pray, and seek God's face for wisdom and knowledge of His word. It's God's desire that we, as His people, be transformed into the image of Christ by the renewing of our mind in His word. Now the word transformed in Romans 12:2 means the same as the word transfigured in Matthew 17:2. Transfigured means a radical change in appearance. There should be a radical change of appearance in our lives when we give our hearts to Jesus Christ and continue to grow into the very image of who He is. It is very important to renew our minds with the Word of God. It will root out any and all evil influences that the devil has planted there that have become a fortress for his lies and could hide and remain unchallenged if we don't. So much of our character remains unchanged because so many of our thoughts remain unchallenged by the Word of God.

And so it was with me. After having experienced a wonderful supernatural presence of God I fell back into the world. I now understand why it is so vital that the character of Christ be seen in us. There are so many people that have gone on and perhaps missed this radical change in their personal lives because of the lack of transformation in our own. However, I want to make a difference. I'm not the only one who feels this way. I realize that there is an army that God is raising up with the same desire.

I left California with an inner desire to be free but driven by a physical lust for the world that was controlled by the devil. As I said before, I had a spiritual war going on inside of me and today while sitting here writing this book, I can tell you that I am very happy to belong to the most high.

To be truthful, the devil had all but completely convinced me that what I was feeling was not wrong, even though I knew in my heart it was. But now I'm realizing that I really needed to give my heart to the Lord. At that time, I was at the beginning of my final plunge to my lowest point of self-esteem. Living in constant fear, rejection and confusion, the thought of taking my life began to resurface. Looking back on my life without God at that time was ugly. There are so many people walking our streets and even in church that try to hide their hurts. That's why in my heart I asked the Father to help me to live my life now to glory His name. Even as a Christian so many times we fall short because of self. As Christians we must realize that our lives belong to Jesus, and we have been bought with a price. I must allow Jesus to use my life the way He now desires. I was lonely and searching for truth that only existed in Jesus Christ. I now live my life and write this book to lift up the name of Jesus Christ and expose the devil. I am determined now more than ever to stand for Christ.

While in the military my job performance as a soldier started to slowly decline. Drinking and using drugs more and more, I became bitter and more hateful. I even disliked myself. I saw no more worth in my existence, and I was consumed by failure. I was slowly losing what little grip I thought I had on my life.

Jesus and the devil were still visiting me and I had no one to turn to, no one to tell what was going on in my life. I remember on one occasion I was in my room lying on my bed. I think I was asleep. I saw a bright light start in the center of the door to the room I was in. I could tell that the light in the door was not life threatening, yet I was afraid of it. I now realize that the light I saw was the light of Christ. It seemed like seconds before the complete entrance of the doorway was filled with that light. Knowing I was afraid, I believed the light left the doorway the same as it had begun.

Now let me explain how I believe in my heart it was Jesus. First it was a bright light-a light that I had never seen before. The light was gentle. It felt peaceful even though I was afraid. The moment that I felt afraid, the light backed away. God is not forceful. He is gentle. Had it been the devil, he would have forced himself on me. The devil uses fear as a weapon to defeat you. So, if it was the devil, seeing me afraid, he would have used it to his advantage.

I know because, there were other demonic experiences that I had before I got saved. Now what

I'm about to say I'm not proud of and only mentioned it to show you the demonic influence of the devil and the power and love of God.

Remember my friend that had been with me from almost the beginning? He and I was starting to give in to our physical desires. Even though we never did anything together, the devil was slowly convincing us that we could be lovers. Now before you begin to kick me, know this. First, God would only let me go but so far. The devil really had me blind, and I was dealing with spirits I had no knowledge of and could not fight. I love my friend still today, but only in the Lord-the true love of God. What excites me now is how Jesus can take my life and use it for His glory. Some might be too ashamed to reveal their lives this way, but I must suffer the persecution in Christ so that someone else can experience the love and deliverance of Christ. Listen, this type of lifestyle is found and tolerated in the Church. Well, I got news for you; this type of lifestyle as well as any lifestyle outside the will of God is sin. Homosexuality is not an alternate lifestyle. It is of the devil, and it is sin. Men and women that practice this lifestyle and don't repent will suffer eternal destruction. That's the word of God!

Well, my life in the military only got harder. I was now a squad leader but was slowly losing my confidence to lead. Don't get me wrong, I was a good soldier and I have the medals and papers to prove it, but I was outside of the will of God for my life and sin was destroying me. I became so bitter and hateful that finally my platoon sergeant approached me about it. He said that my job performance was dropping and that he noticed that I was hateful toward everyone including him. Well of course I denied it but in my heart, I knew he was right.

Let me back up a moment, I was in another platoon before my superiors sent me to another platoon hoping the change would do me some good. Before changing platoons, my superiors at that time were going to send me to a hospital in Germany to dry out. In other words, to help me to stop drinking. I refused to go and I said that if they made me go they could have my discharge papers ready for me when I got back. Truly, I was a mess. I remember just breaking down into tears when I was alone.

Needless to say, they didn't send me. They only transferred me from one platoon to another. That's when, after a while, my other platoon sergeant approached me about my behavior. He told me that he and his superiors thought I needed to see a psychiatrist. I went off!! Listen, people can see what we often overlook about ourselves. So, I asked him did he think I was going crazy? He said no, but you do have a problem that is deeper than the surface. He said I've watched you become worse and worse. That's when I agreed to go.

When I agreed to go, he told me good and made the appointment the same day. Even though I agreed to go I was hurt. I went that afternoon and talked with a doctor that lasted about a half hour. Let me show you how God orders our footsteps. The psychiatrist that I talked with was a born-again Christian. He told me I was running from God. I thank God for this man today.

After the meeting I left his office to return back to my unit. Before I could get back, my platoon sergeant had called and told my superior I was on the verge on a nervous breakdown. Beloved the Bible says:

> *The thief comes only in order to steal and kill and destroy. I came that they may have and enjoy life, and have it in abundance (to the full, till it [a]overflows).* John 10:10

Here Jesus was letting the Jews know His mission and the devil's mission. At this stage of my life, the devil had stolen my identity, had killed my self-esteem, and finally he was trying to destroy me. My platoon sergeant met me in his office and told me to go and pack my things because he was sending me back to the hospital. That was almost the final blow. Satan had one more blow that he thought would take me out-but it didn't. it wasn't God's plan.

I did as he said and packed all my things. I went to the hospital where I stayed a week. Because I was on the verge of a nervous breakdown, they gave me something to bring me down mentally. While I was there some of the young soldiers that I was originally in the platoon with came to see me. They gave me a card and a flower and told me how much they cared.

I was an infantryman, and we went to the field to train a lot. But because of the nervous breakdown they thought I was about to have they left me behind to get better. They had put me on a 30-day approval leave of absence. After getting out of the hospital, I stayed straight for about two weeks. I went back to drinking again but little did I know God was about to make His move in salvation for me. I started drinking with my friends again as I said, and I was getting depressed all over again. While with some friends drinking one night, I thought I heard someone outside the room that I was in call me by my nickname, "Butch". I stopped what I was doing, and I asked everyone did they hear someone call me. They all said no. Except one person who started laughing at me and said, "you are nothing but an alcoholic, you haven't heard anything." But I was sure I heard someone call me.

I decided to go back to the room where I was living and the one guy that had made fun of me agreed to take me back. While on the way back he apologized and said, "I believe you". But by then, I was next to tears and told him he was right. I was nothing but an alcoholic.

When I got to the building I walked around to the front door. I had planted the flower that the soldiers gave me outside in front of the building. As I walked passed the flower I noticed that it was turning yellow and dying. Right then the Lord spoke to my heart and said, "you are just like that plant; you're dying". He then asked me "what do I have to do to make you serve me"? Well, I started crying and went and stood in the mirror and said to myself, "I don't like you anymore." Before that night was over the devil tried to convince me to jump out a window and kill myself because my life was over.

I went to the bed, laid down, and fell to sleep. I woke up the following morning and Satan was right there waiting for me. As I opened my eyes and began to bring my thoughts together, he interrupted my thought process with his voice trying to get me to go downtown and start drinking all over again. I had money in my pocket and I was still on approved leave. However, I spoke out loud so my own ears could hear and I told him "no". I told him that I was tired of getting drunk and killing myself. Now, just as I refused to allow the devil to come in and control me again, I instantly heard the voice of Jesus say to me "get up and follow Me." Yes He spoke to my heart and told me to get up and follow Him just like He told the disciples.

All of a sudden I heard chains fall from me. I leaped to my feet and stood erect in the bed. Jesus brought to memory another friend that had tried to witness to me before. I quickly got some clothes on and raced to where he was working. As I was on the way to his workplace Satan had placed people in my path. They were people I was friends with, and they offered me drugs and alcohol but I would not stop- not for one minute. I told them no. I had something else to do and I kept going. The devil was hoping

I would stop and give him a conversation and thus have a chance to change my mind. I've learned and I'm still learning that you can't give the devil the time of day. If you give him anything, give him the Word of God. That's the only thing that he listens to. He is powerless against the Word of God. As I said, the devil had placed people in front of me the same hour to try and stop what was about to happen. He knew he was about to lose ground and that ground was me.

I can't remember his name, but I went to his workplace, and he remembered me. I told him what I was there for, and he got really excited about my decision. He told me to meet him at his barracks at 12 o'clock for lunch because he wanted me to meet his Pastor. Yes, God has Pastors everywhere, even in the military. I'm talking about Pastors after His own heart, Holy Spirit filled people.

I met him, and from his barracks we went to a civilian cafeteria. I will never forget that moment or the pastor and his wife. We met in the cafeteria, and we sat in a booth in the back where there was hardly any light and I renounced the devil and accepted Jesus Christ as my personal savior right there. As I said it was a moment I would never forget, and I hope someday to see them again before I leave the earth. From that precious moment my life was never the same. I left that place with all guilt of sin lifted from me. I was a new person.

> *Therefore if any person is [ingrafted] in Christ (the Messiah) he is a new creation (a new creature altogether); the old [previous moral and spiritual condition] has passed away. Behold, the fresh and new has come!* 2 Corinthians 5:17

Spiritually I was a new man. Christ had now come into my heart to rule. I was now a child of God. Old things had passed away. The Greek for old is "archaios' meaning ancient, original or old. Such things are in me no more. I had been reconciled back to God. In it reads:

> *For if while we were enemies we were reconciled to God through the death of His Son, it is much more [certain], now that we are reconciled, that we shall be saved (daily delivered from sin's dominion) through His [[a] resurrection] life.* Romans 5:10

Did you hear that child of God? You are, as a child of God, being daily delivered from sin's dominion. That's wonderful news! The power of Christ is constantly working in you and me bringing us into the image of who He is when you truly belong to Him. As a child of the most high you are now the righteousness of God in Christ.

I can remember walking down the sidewalk one day and I stopped in my tracks. I thought to myself

"I'm not swearing". I had been totally set free from using profanity. I had become a new creature. At that moment I realized that before I accepted Christ I was under the complete influence of Satan. An evil spirit of destruction drove me. I no longer used profanity, drank, or used drugs. From those things I had been instantly set free. Jesus had given me joy that words could not express. I remember running out of that cafeteria and running to the first person I saw, which happened to be a middle-aged white woman and told her about Jesus setting me free. She looked at me and smiled and said, "good for you." The joy that Jesus had given me, I had to tell everyone and anyone I met.

Well, I joined the Church that the minister was from and I grew spiritually. One Sunday after church, we all went to one of the member's houses for dinner. While there, some of the members started talking about the baptism of the Holy Ghost. Not really knowing exactly what they were speaking of I said that I was saved. And another one said, "yes, you got saved by the holy spirit and the power of God changed you when you accepted Jesus Christ as your savior, however, you must ask for the baptism of the Holy Spirit as found in Luke 11:13."

> *If you then, evil as you are, know how to give good gifts [gifts [a]that are to their advantage] to your children, how much more will your heavenly Father give the Holy Spirit to those*

who ask and [h]continue to ask Him! Luke 11:13

When I realized that I did not have the baptism of the Holy Spirit I was crushed.

But to as many as did receive and welcome Him, He gave the authority (power, privilege, right) to become the children of God, that is, to those who believe in (adhere to, trust in, and rely on) His name— John 1:12

That's what happened to me and other Christians that believe and rely on the name of Jesus for salvation. You receive power, the privilege and the ability to become children of God. But as seen in Luke 11:13, you must ask for the baptism of the Holy Ghost. The word "power" in John 1:12, in the Greek, means "exousia." It is delegated power, the right and liberty to use power. It is the liberty and right for every man to be saved. However, in Acts 1:8 the word "power", in the Greek, means "dunamis"-inherited power capable of reproducing itself like a dynamo. It means ability, strength, might, mighty, miracle, and worker of miracles. The baptism of the Holy Spirit is what gives power to the believer to live like Christ and do the works of Christ.

And when Jesus was baptized, He went up at once out of the water; and behold, the heavens

> *were opened, and he [John] saw the Spirit of God descending like a dove and alighting on Him.* Matthew 3:16

> *For John baptized with water, but not many days from now you shall be baptized with (*[a] *placed in, introduced into) the Holy Spirit.* Acts 1:5

> *But you shall receive power (ability, efficiency, and might) when the Holy Spirit has come upon you, and you shall be My witnesses in Jerusalem and all Judea and Samaria and to the ends (the very bounds) of the earth.* Acts 1:8

First of all, Jesus told the disciples that they would receive power to be witnesses after they received the baptism of the Holy Spirit. They already believed on His name. They received the power to not only be verbal witnesses of Christ, but also to do the works of Christ.

Now some believe and teach that all the disciples, God did not fill people with the Holy Spirit. I don't' believe that because I know what happened to me. Also, why would Jesus say in Luke 11:13 the Father would give the Holy Spirit (His Spirit) to anyone who asked Him, if He knew the disciples would be the only ones to receive it? As I said, I was hurt when I found out that I had not received the baptism of the Holy Spirit. So much so, that as I walked home that night I was talking to God about receiving the baptism of the Holy Spirit.

Well, some two or three weeks later, after church, we went to another house for dinner. While there, someone gave me a book titled "The Holy Spirit and You." While sitting down in the front room of the house reading the book, the Minister that led me to Christ asked me had I received the baptism of the Holy Spirit. Still disappointed: I said, "no". Then he asked me was I ready to receive the baptism of the Holy Spirit, I said "yes!" To be sure, he asked me again and I said exactly the same thing. "Yes!" He then asked the owner of the house could we use one of their rooms upstairs to pray. Of course, they said yes and we went upstairs and my life changed again forever.

The minister and his wife led me into a small bedroom upstairs and shut the door. He then told me to get down on my knees next to the bed and pray. As he stood over me, his wife went and stood at a window that was shut. In fact, it was the only window in the room.

I began to pray, and I asked God to fill me with the Holy Spirit. As I prayed the minister that stood over me prayed and said, "God, I'm not letting him up until he is filled with the Holy Spirit." Instantly my mind said God you got to hurry up because my knees are hurting. After praying and asking God to fill me, the minister told me to start giving the highest praise. He asked me did I know what that was, and I said "no". He then said, "Hallelujah is the highest praise." I started giving God that praise as hard as I could.

As I praised God from my heart, something wonderful happened. I will never forget that day as long as I live. While on my knees praying and praising God, a gentle wind past over me and I began to speak in another tongue or heavenly language. At first, I was a little afraid and I stopped by just shutting my mouth and not speaking. But the minister said, "don't be afraid, just allow the Holy Spirit to take control." What I found out through personal experience is that He (the Holy Spirit) is very gentle. He would not force His way. He manifested His presence through that heavenly language as I gave way to Him.

I like what the King James Version has to say in the book of Acts.

> *And when the day of Pentecost was fully come, they were all with one accord in one place.* –
> Acts 2:1

Chapter one of Acts tells us that there were about a hundred and twenty people gathered together and they were all in one accord. None was there uninterested, unconcern, or lukewarm. They all were in earnest and united in faith and prayer. Did you hear that? They were all there united in faith. They were all there with expectation.

There are so many people today that go to Church but really not hungry for God. There are a lot of reasons why people go to Church and to the particular Church they attend. I don't care what church you go to, if you are not there searching for God, longing for God, you will not find Him.

> *Blessed and fortunate and happy and [a] spiritually prosperous (in that state in which the born-again child of God [b]enjoys His favor and salvation) are those who hunger and thirst for righteousness (uprightness and right standing with God), for they shall be [c] completely satisfied!* Matt. 5:6

> *Blessed are the pure in heart: for they shall see God.* Matthew 5:8

The Greek word for "pure" is "katharos", translated clean.

> *For He knew who was going to betray Him, that was the reason He said, not all of you are clean.* John 13:11

The word clean here also means pure in heart. Jesus knows every one of us. He also knows the motives of our heart. While you can look right to man, God knows, sees, and understands the heart. There is a lot of mess that people bring to God or call themselves bringing to God. They come to church, but they are not willing to let it go, and they don't see the manifestation of God in that area of their lives. This verse also refers to the new birth that we experience when we accept Jesus Christ as our savior.

> *Therefore if anyone is in Christ [that is, grafted in, joined to Him by faith in Him as Savior], he is a new creature [reborn and renewed by the Holy Spirit]; the old things [the previous moral and spiritual condition] have passed away. Behold, new things have come [because spiritual awakening brings a new life].* 2 Corinthians 5:17

We need to look at this because I said people come to church for so many wrong reasons, we don't see the power of the Holy Spirit manifest as He may want to because we grieve Him.

However, I received the Holy Spirit similar to the way it is read in Acts.

> *And suddenly there came a sound from heaven as of a rushing mighty wind, and it filled all the house where they were sitting.* Acts 2:2

As I stated earlier, a gentle wind blew over me and through the room where I was. Church, this is real. The devil has a lot of people out there saying that God doesn't do this anymore. That's a lie. God is filling people and baptizing people in the Holy Spirit today. The church needs to wake up and walk in the power that's been given to them. Like I said, my life was changed forever.

As I will share with you in the next chapter, I was surprised to know how many people, and who they were, that would refuse the truth. The devil tried to convince me that what I experienced was not real. I knew what I had experienced was real and He has been working in me and in my life bringing me to my purpose for God in the earth. He will do the same thing for you.

Listen, you cannot be led into the truth except the Holy Spirit does it. That's why so many people are so confused today. There are a lot of counterfeits in the body of Christ. Satan has for a season, successfully placed some people in the body of Christ as leaders that don't have the spirit of the living God. I'm not judging people but listen, if you don't have the spirit of God in your life, someone who doesn't have the Spirit of God in his or her life will mislead you. This is what has happened with a lot of people.

Before I close this chapter, let's look at one more thing. Many people have relied on their ability to live for God and do the works of Christ that He has ordained the Church to do. You cannot live for God or do what Christ has commissioned the Church to do without the power and presence of the Holy Spirit.

And I will ask the Father, and He will give you another Comforter (Counselor, Helper, Intercessor, Advocate, Strengthener, and Standby), that He may remain with you forever. John 14:16

Look at all the things the Holy Spirit is for you as a believer. I leap for joy to know that I have someone so wonderful on my side and that actually lives inside of me to make me into what God wants me to be.

> *But the Comforter (Counselor, Helper, Intercessor, Advocate, Strengthener, Standby), the Holy Spirit, Whom the Father will send in My name [in My place, to represent Me and act on My behalf], He will teach you all things. And He will cause you to recall (will remind you of, bring to your remembrance) everything I have told you.* John 14:26

So church, as you can see, you need the Holy Spirit. Child of God you need the Spirit of Truth (the Holy Spirit) to see and walk in the truth. Look at what else Jesus said.

> *However, I am telling you nothing but the truth when I say it is profitable (good, expedient, advantageous) for you that I go away. Because if I do not go away, the Comforter (Counselor, Helper, Advocate, Intercessor, Strengthener, Standby) will not come to you [into close fellowship with you]; but if I go away, I will send Him to you [to be in close fellowship with you].* John 16:7

> *But when He, the Spirit of Truth (the Truth-giving Spirit) comes, He will guide you into all the Truth (the whole, full Truth). For He will not speak His own message [on His own authority]; but He will tell whatever He hears [from the Father; He will give the message that has been given to Him], and He will announce and declare to you the things that are to come [that will happen in the future]. He will honor and glorify Me, because He will take of (receive, draw upon) what is Mine and will reveal (declare, disclose, transmit) it to you.* John 16:13-14

I wonder sometimes just how many people have died in the sin of hatred because they thought they were right. Someone will give an account for the lies that they told someone else and that lie led them into hell.

I believe that part of the problem is that people try to represent God through themselves and not by the Holy Spirit. Thus, they transmit to others their own thoughts and ideas. That my friend is of the flesh and will lead people into greater bondage. Satan doesn't want you to know that you can be filled with the Holy Spirit. Beloved, not only can you receive the Baptism of the Holy Spirit, but also you need the Spirit of Truth to guide you. If you have accepted Christ as your Savior, stop now, and ask Him for the Baptism of the Holy Spirit. He promised you and me a Comforter, Counselor, Helper, Intercessor, Advocate, Strengthener and Standby. Receive power from on high today. Victory belongs to you.

CHAPTER
FIVE

"I WENT TO MY OWN, AND MY OWN RECEIVED ME NOT"

Just before leaving Italy God revealed two other things to me. One was His glory, and the other was what I was about to face.

Well, every day after work I would run back to where I was living to get with God. He was coming to me in dreams and had manifested Himself to me so much that I had to learn to walk with Him by faith and trust Him to know He was there. Of course, I later learned in His word that Jesus promised to never leave us. He told me that Satan could also reveal himself as an angel of light and His word also confirms that.

> *And it is no wonder, for Satan himself masquerades as an angel of light.* 2 Corinthians 11:14

One afternoon after work I ran home excited about getting into God's presence and expecting something from Him. I got there and I took a bath and went back in my room to dry off and dress. As I was drying off, He spoke to me and said, "Don't wait to dress to get into my presence come now because I see you and not what you have on. I see you the way you are with or without clothes." Now don't take that as a spiritual move for you to try something. I realize now He was telling me not let things stop me from coming to Him. Don't wait, but come now, just as you are.

Well, that's exactly what I did. He led me to cover any light that was in the room and coming through the window. After doing that, I got on my knees and started talking to God. I crouched over as I was praying, and I asked Him to let me see His glory. The Holy Spirit then asked me did I believe He would. I said yes. He then asked me gain did I believe He would, I said yes again. The Holy Spirit told me to sit up. As I sat up, the room became bright with a light that I really can't explain. The Holy Spirit cried out through me and said, "Jesus is Lord!" Just as that happened I crouched back over and after that the light of God's presence left the room. Yes, this is true. He literally lit the room up with the light of His presence. Many people don't' believe that God does things like that anymore, but He does. God is just as real now and willing to show Himself to man as He was then. All He wants is a people that desire Him that much.

You may ask yourself, "Is that biblical?" Yes, it is.

And Moses said, I beseech You, show me Your glory. And God said, I will make all My goodness pass before you, and I will proclaim My name, THE LORD, before you; for I will be gracious to whom I will be gracious, and will show mercy and loving-kindness on whom I will show mercy and loving-kindness. Exodus 33:18-19

This is the only reason I can tell you why God did that for me. It's because of what His word says in these verses. He will be gracious, and He will show loving-kindness to whom He will show loving-kindness.

The second thing that God revealed to me was the condition of the church that I was going back to. He came in a dream and showed me walking toward the Church. As I was walking to the front of the church I saw people running out of the church. I tried to stop some of them to ask why they were running out of the church, but I couldn't. Finally, He led me to the back of the church, and He showed me why people were leaving out of the church. There He showed me a principality that was ruling the church.

Well, needless to say after I got home, I walked right into warfare that I did not understand. In returning home I had to live with my parents because I came home with nothing. While in the military, I had thrown all but about 10 months of 6 ½ years away to the devil. Being single I should have had something to show for the years I spent in the Army, but I had nothing. I remember feeling ashamed and did not want to come home, but the Lord told me to go home because He had already planned out my life. I got off track some but God through His infinite wisdom and power got me back on track, which I will share later.

I thought that me coming home, saved and filled with the Holy Spirit, would be the thing that family and friends would want to see. However, Satan had planned an attack of his own. Coming back to a Baptist home and church, after being away for 6 ½ years, I found that things really had not changed much at all. It caused a lot of trouble for me, which, at the time, I could not understand. Some of my family and friends thought I was crazy.

In the sixth chapter of the book of Ephesians it tells us that we wrestle not against flesh and blood. Our enemy is spiritual. But being young in the Lord at that time, I did not know how to combat the enemy.

At church, they allowed me to teach one Sunday, and to me they seemed to have enjoyed it. So much so they asked me to start a Bible study at the church one night a week. Little did I know that it was a set-up by the devil to beat me up. I started the Biblestudy and little by little people started to come. What I didn't realize at that time was I was not ready to teach anyone the Word of God the way it needed to be taught. I was a baby in Christ and the devil knew it.

Study and be eager and do your utmost to present yourself to God approved (tested by

> *trial), a workman who has no cause to be ashamed, correctly analyzing and accurately dividing [rightly handling and skillfully teaching] the Word of Truth.* 2 Tim. 2:15

Being a babe in Christ, only ten months old in the Lord, I had no idea that it was a scheme-a crafty plot of the devil to get me eaten alive by people that really thought they knew God, and that's exactly what happened.

> *I bear them witness that they have a [certain] zeal and enthusiasm for God, but it is not enlightened and according to [correct and vital] knowledge.* Romans 10:2

While I was on the right path being born again and baptized in the Holy Spirit, I was yet a babe in Christ and lacked vital teaching.

> *Behold, I am sending you out like sheep in the midst of wolves; be [a]wary and wise as serpents, and be innocent (harmless, guileless, and [b]without falsity) as doves.* Matthew 10:16

Plus, I did not know my enemy.

> *Be well balanced (temperate, sober of mind), be vigilant and cautious at all times; for that enemy of yours, the devil, roams around like*

> *a lion roaring [[a]in fierce hunger], seeking someone to seize upon and devour.* 1 Peter 5:8

Listen the devil stands back and studies the weak and unfortified areas in our lives-areas not built up in the word. He attacks with quiet and tricky moves. This is why many times we never recognize our enemy until he has already established a foothold in our lives. As a Christian you must wise up to the devil's trickery. However, that was not the only time the enemy tricked me. There would be other times. There would be many spiritual battles I would have to fight, even in the home of my parents before leaving. After stiff resistance from family and members of my home church, I soon gave up the Bible study. However, I remained a member of the church and I joined the choir. By now I was grieved in my spirit and felt alone many times, but the Lord gave me the strength to stand.

One Sunday, while in the choir, the spirit of God came upon me, and I stood up while the offering was being received and spoke out. Under the influence of the Holy Spirit, I said: "You need to seek God's face." The Holy Spirit spoke through me and said to the people: "You don't know me, and you never knew me."

I guess you can imagine how that went over. I was already not the most popular person in the church. They really didn't have much to say to me then. I then started asking God to move me.

It had really hit me now that they would not receive me. I then remembered by the Holy Spirit what the scriptures said about our Savior.

He came to that which belonged to Him [to His own—His domain, creation, things, world], and they who were His own did not receive Him and did not welcome Him. John 1:11

My own people had rejected me. I no longer felt welcomed where I was born and raised. And the time would come that I would eventually leave.

I could feel the resistance from everyone I got around. One of my sisters would later tell me that she deliberately avoided me because she knew she was not saved, but went to church, and because of the things people and family was saying about me. People that said they loved God but was showing hostility and ill treatment toward me were persecuting me. I was being bombarded by many questions that at that time I could not answer. I was sometimes afraid to get around them.

Because Jesus was my conversation, it was said that I had lost my mind. Well, to be quite honest, Jesus had blown my mind. I had fallen in love with my creator and what a wonderful feeling it was.

That Sunday, after I sat down, the Pastor of the church at that time stood up and said that before that church became holy, he would have the doors pad locked. OH, what a stupid statement that was.

Because of his statement some of the members later left the church after I did. The church rejected God and God rejected them. To this day that church is still dead.

There was a third thing that I must now mention. Just before leaving Italy God again came to me in a dream and showed how He would shake the earth off of its axes. Large boulders or objects would fall from the sky and mankind, as a whole would still walk away from Him into darkness. Because I was a young Christian at that time, I told the man that God was using to help establish me in the Word and my relationship with God. He took me to the 16th chapter of Revelation, which I was unfamiliar with at that time. In this chapter it speaks of the seventh vial.

> *Then the seventh [angel] emptied out his bowl into the air, and a mighty voice came out of the sanctuary of heaven from the throne [of God], saying, It is done! [It is all over, it is all accomplished, it has come!] And there followed lightning flashes, loud rumblings, peals of thunder, and a tremendous earthquake; nothing like it has ever occurred since men dwelt on the earth, so severe and far-reaching was that earthquake. The mighty city was broken into three parts, and the cities of the nations fell. And God kept in mind mighty Babylon, to make her drain the cup of His furious wrath and indignation. And every island fled*

> *and no mountains could be found. And great (excessively oppressive) hailstones, as heavy as a talent [between fifty and sixty pounds], of immense size, fell from the sky on the people; and men blasphemed God for the plague of the hail, so very great was [the torture] of that plague.* Rev. 16:17-21 (also read Isaiah 66:6)

In 1984 God came and showed me all of this. I did not know all that God had called me to, but today it is unfolding little by little. Today we, as God's people, must lie before God to receive instruction and not just follow man-made methods and ideas that God has not called us to. We must wake up and live in Christ so that Christ and His character can be revealed in us.

As I read and study the Book of Ezekiel, I see flashes of the church. In this book of the bible, Judah had left God to serve man-made images. This in return angered God and brought about the fall of Judah. Today the church relies on methods to grow a church physically, not that there is anything wrong with that, but we must not lose focus on how and where the church is growing Spiritually. We as God's people must return to our first love. Stop running after what God has in His hand. Instead, run after what God has in His heart. God desires from His people true love and worship. Look at what Jesu said to the Samaritan woman.

> *You (Samaritans) do not know what you are worshiping (you worship what you do not comprehend). We do know what we are worshiping (we worship what we have knowledge of and understanding, for (after all) salvation comes from (among) the Jews. A time will come, however, indeed it is already here, when the true (genuine) worshipers will worship the father in spirit and in truth (reality); for the Father is seeking just such people as these as His worshipers.* John 4:22-23.

Today, in this country, many churches have become their own god. They reject truth and rely on the wisdom of the flesh. As I stated earlier, only the Holy Spirit can reveal all of what Christ is. Look at what the Word says.

> *Now when Jesus went into the region of Caesarea Philippi, He asked His disciples, who do people say that he Son of Man is? And they answered, some say John the Baptist; others say Elijah; and others Jeremiah or one of the prophets* – Matthew 16:13-14.

Stop! Doesn't that sound like people who go to church today? While they might not give the answers that the disciples gave to Jesus; there are people that really don't know if they are saved. But they go to church. Others don't believe the word of God, but they go to church. And still, there are others who are just following the crowd. There are still many people that say and believe other things.

> *He said to them, but who do you (yourselves) say that I am? Simon Peter replied, You are the Christ, the Son of the living God. Then Jesus answered him, Blessed (happy, fortunate, and to be envied) are you, Simon Bar-Jonah. For flesh and blood (men) have not revealed this to you, but my Father who is in heaven –* Matthew 16:15-17

As much as I dislike saying this, there are many who no longer seek God for revelation. Instead, they try to understand that which is Spirit with the natural mind and fail to see God. Look at what the word says:

> *That way is born of the flesh and what is born of the spirit is spirit. Then He said marvel not at what I said, because you must be born anew from above.* John 3:6-7

Listen Body of Christ; during the time I was writing this chapter of this book, God came to me in a dream. During the dream, I saw a man standing in the midst of a crowd of people. He was speaking out to them saying, "Jesus is fresh oil, Jesus is fresh oil, Jesus is fresh oil." I believe that Jesus is about to pour out of His Spirit a fresh anointing on the Body of Christ. Don't miss it. CATCH THE ANOINTING.

CHAPTER SIX

"GOD ORDERS THE FOOTSTEPS OF THE RIGHTEOUS"

Learning to walk with God takes time. Learning to hear His voice takes time. You getting in a hurry will not make God get in a hurry or change His desires for your life. That's something I learned the hard way.

After coming home and not being accepted, it appeared that I had become a little confused. I've learned now, of course, that there are times you have to be still and wait on God. At that time, although saved, I had not learned to fully listen to the voice of God. All I knew at that time was I needed to get out of the atmosphere I was in.

As I said in Chapter 5, I started crying out to God. My earthly father later told me that I needed to go to school. I agreed with him and started looking for a school to attend. We all must be taught the

Bible and how to walk with God. What we have to be careful of is who we learn from and what we learn.

It was later decided that I should attend a school of divinity in my local area, the name of which I will disclose. At that time, I was confused and did not know what direction to go in nor had I developed a prayer life. So, I decided to go to the school that had been mentioned to me.

As I began to get everything in order to go to school, the Holy Spirit revealed to me that this was not God's intended purpose for me. God had already chosen the man He wanted me to sit under and learn from. It was not the traditional setting and direction that He wanted me to go in. Now I had to tell my dad that this school was not God's plan for me, and that He had already chosen the way for me. To my surprise my daddy accepted the decision and left it alone. However, it would still be some time before I would see God's plan for me unfold.

I don't like saying what I'm about to write but I must obey God. Just before leaving home again to learn how to follow God's intended purpose for my life, God revealed something to me. As a young man and still a babe in Christ, He told me from the book of Daniel that He had called me as a prophet to this nation. He would later reveal to me that the ministry He had called me to would not manifest until later. The Body of Christ will go through a cleansing, and we will learn to run after God, as a people, with our whole heart.

As I said in the beginning of this chapter, learning to walk with God takes time and is very vital. There are so many people out there that, I believe, are earnest in their desire to serve God but have become overly anxious and thus wandered off into their own will and desire for their lives instead of waiting for God to make them. Unless you have someone to teach you how to wait and why you should wait you will become self-made and self-promoted. If there is a true call and true anointing on your life, you need not worry. It will come to pass.

I learned some things the hard way because I wanted things my way. Doing things my way led to years of more confusion and hurt. I knew I had a call from God but not knowing how to wait for God's leading I did what most people do. I sat down and came up with my own plan and then asked God to bless it. This doesn't work.

Listen, the devil as I've said before is very crafty. Satan knows exactly how to pull you out of God's will to leave you vulnerable to his plan of attack. God had told me things that He was going to do in my life, but I didn't wait for Him and later created a mess for Him to fix.

I mentioned that God had called me as a prophet to this nation. I was afraid to tell people what God had called me to be because of a fear of rejection. I realized now that no matter what the circumstances may be, I must rise to the call and tell the people what

God has shown me about this nation. But, I had to learn all this in my growth and walk with Him.

A few months later, still at home, I met a pretty young lady who would become my first wife. Yes, I've been divorced and will go into more detail about that, the healing that had to take place, and the lies that the devil tried to tell me about how it was over for me because God wouldn't forgive me. Satan also used Christians to tell me this. It was a very painful experience, but God brought me through it.

Before I go on about my marriage to this young woman, let me say again that God had spoken to me about things He was going to do in my life and one of those things was to give me a son.

Now I had prayed about getting married, but I was young and not willing to wait on God. But meeting this young woman was how I learned about a wonderful man of God, that God had chosen for me to learn from. However, I saw something else also I wanted. This young lady was saved and was already in school under this anointed man of God.

I started going to the church she attended and later joined this church after we were united in marriage. I learned the hard way about learning to listen to God. In all honesty, I except full responsibility for the dissolution of my first marriage, because I believed that God had laid on my heart to wait. However, I chose not to.

I can remember in my heart, the voice I believe was God telling me to wait. I even said to my brother (older family member) that I was going to ask God to go to plan B, instead of plan A. Well, what I learned from that experience was God will not change His plan because you don't like it. I wanted God to join in with me and do what I wanted Him to do like so many other people do today. God is not going to join your plan (mess); you must learn to follow God and His will for your life. You will avoid a lot of trouble if you just get and stay in God's will and wait on Him to lead your heart. That's all in the learning process of walking with God.

As I said, I later joined the church and began to grow spiritually. I married into a family. She had two young girls who I adopted and gave my name. They are my children. We would later have the son God had told me about.

Let me pause here for a moment to say this. The Bible teaches us not to be unequally yoked.

> *Do not be unequally yoked with unbeliever [do not make mismated alliances with them or come under a different yoke with them, inconsistent with your faith]. For what partnership have right living and right standing with God with iniquity and lawlessness? Or how can light have fellowship with darkness?* – 2 Cor. 6:14

The part that I want to focus on is the part in parenthesis. Do not make mismated alliances with them or come under a different yoke with them. What

I learned later in life that you can be unequally yoked in faith and purpose.

As I said before, I accepted full responsibility and I reaped what I sowed. It was not my intended purpose to hurt anyone. I learned that following my desires, even as a Christian, and not the will of God can bring hurt to others.

There are so many ways that Satan can lead babes in Christ even older Christians out of the will of God if they are not taught how to be still as the Lord makes them vessels of honor. Being overly anxious for anything can lead to trouble. As I grew in the Lord under this great man of God, I began to realize what I had done. As a few more years came and passed my spirit became heavy because of what I saw coming but did not want to accept. At one point, I even prayed to God about me not doing what He had called me to do. I feared more than anything going to my grave and I had not obeyed the call. I think at one point the call became something I was not sure of. I knew that God was not a God of separation and divorce. So why was it happening to me? I knew that I had the call before I got married. For some of you, perhaps, you have no idea what it is like to see your marriage falling apart as you pray for others.

There were days when my first wife would take all the children and go to her mothers because I had to work. The moment they drove away from the house I would fall on my knees in tears asking God for mercy. I remember asking God to judge me, even if it meant dying, but let my family live and be safe. I knew I had sinned and it wasn't their fault. I did tell my first wife from the very start what God had called me to do, and I was sure she would follow me. But when I knew that the time had come for me to obey God, she wouldn't do it. I really learned a hard lesson about waiting on God. Even to this day I still must bear the burden of what it had done to my children. God healed them and we all have gone on an have a good relationship to this day. Two of them have even come to understand why things happened the way they did.

God at that time had come to me in so many dreams that I will not even try to put them all into this book. Only the dreams that He brought back to me have I written about in this book.

Well, before my first wife and I separated, God confirmed in me the call of a a Prophet. I was reluctant to share this because so many people were already claiming to be this and that and yet people were and still are being misled. Understand this, obedience comes before blessing. There are so many people in the Body of Christ that just want the blessings of God but not the responsibility of righteousness. There are many people that don't desire God to work His will in their lives to make them children or rather disciples for Him. They just want the reward for looking like a Christian and really not becoming one.

Anyway, I said that God confirmed His call in my life. He did this by first dropping it into my spirit. He later confirmed it with the Pastor that I sat under.

The Pastor did not know me that well then, and I had not told anyone of my call as a Prophet. I went up for prayer one Sunday and I honestly didn't go for a word from God. In fact, it wasn't even on my mind. But when I left my seat and went up for prayer I believe the Holy Spirit used my Pastor to confirm the call. Even then I did not try to step out but I sat still and allowed God to teach me through this man of God. It has been twenty years and now God is telling me now is the time to tell this nation what I saw.

Before I lose this thought let me share this with you. God is a forgiving God. I paid the price for not listening to God. He forgave me and He healed me as well as all the others involved. For a while as I mentioned earlier, I thought perhaps it was over for me. But as I showed you in the scriptures earlier Jesus said that all manner of sin is forgiven to man but one, and that is blasphemy against the Holy Spirit. So even if you've made mistakes, you are forgiven, go and sin no more. That's what Jesus said. Listen all you have to do is ask for forgiveness and sin no more there is one other thing, you must forgive yourself and then live on in victory.

Let me say this also. For you married couples; learn to walk in the call of God together and respect the call on your mate whether it is on the wife or the husband. Ask God to help you to follow your husband or wife as they follow Christ. Honor God and He will honor you.

Just before my first wife and divorced God came to me in a dream. I know without a doubt this dream was from the Lord. He showed me and my first wife walking in a jungle. My wife was running ahead of me, and I was trying to catch her. I called to her to wait for me and she would not. As she ran ahead of me, I saw her come to a table with a serpent on it. Another man was standing by the table watching over the snake. As my wife approached the table the man told her to rub the snake on the head. While running to her I saw this and screamed out, "don't touch the snake." However, she did and the snake bit down into her hand. When I got to the table, I took my wife by the wrist of her hand the snake had bitten into and grabbed the snake by the back of the head. As I began to try to pull the fangs out of her hand I awoke from the dream.

When I came out of my sleep the Holy Spirit laid on my heart to tell my wife to walk with me and not ahead of me. If not, the marriage would suffer for it. I did as the Lord said. I woke my wife and told her what the Lord had told me and she then went back to sleep. I know it's hard to believe but it's true.

As time went on, I lost my joy as a Christian and my wife began to see the frustration that disobedience brought me. I cried a lot in that relationship, asking God to help me. It was my disobedience from the beginning that brought all this hurt. Had I listened when He told me to wait all this could have been avoided. I wish I could tell you why things work out the way they do. But all I can say is that He brought us all through.

Still, after receiving confirmation about my call from God and through the Pastor, I waited. I kept praying and asking God to help me. I was still afraid to believe what God had chosen for me to do. I believe somewhere in the mid to late 1980's He came to me in a dream about terrorism. I can't remember the name of the person that Satan was using then as a terrorist, but I do remember what God showed me in the dream.

Reagan was the President at the time and God told me that President Reagan would send aircraft overseas to bomb this terrorist group that existed in the 1980's. God showed me that for a while terrorism would die down to nothing but years later would rise again to be even worse. Of course, not knowing who to tell for fear of rejection and looking crazy I didn't tell a soul.

Now, I know that it has already happened, and it would be easy for me to write about something that has already taken place. But I can only do what God has put on my heart to do. This is true. God showed it to me before it happened. You might say, why me? I don't know except for the fact that He showed it to me. God showed me other things that have happened and showed me things that are to happen.

I believe God did that to confirm for me the call He had placed on my life and to build the confidence I needed in Him. He also showed me in the late 1980's that there would be a President in the country that would need more protection than any President before him. Well during the inauguration of President Bush (the son) an announcer during the ceremony said that this President would need more protection than any President before him. Believe it or not, God showed me that before it happened. In fact, in one particular church service, the Pastor said the same thing in his sermon confirming what the Lord had showed me. God came to me in dream after dream about this country being attacked on its own soil. The same dream over and over.

In the dream I saw myself running from what appeared to me to be spaceships. They were flying over America dropping bombs everywhere. Night after night I would have the same dream. As I ran for shelter, I could not understand why I could not recognize these funny looking aircraft. Then it finally came to me. They were foreign aircraft from another country. I believe God was showing me that this country would be attacked on its own soil by foreign aircraft. Does another country have the capability of doing this? I don't know about now, but one day they might.

God also came to me about our country being threatened again at our borders. In this dream I asked one of the soldiers where they were going? He replied saying: "We are going to the borders of our country because of a threat there." Do I believe this is real? Yes. Everything else has come to pass and I believe this will too.

I have kept all these dreams to myself until now. I said before that I would ask God when I could share all the things, He had shown me and all the experiences that I had with Him. Now is the time. It is time for America to fall on her knees and repent of her sins and turn wholly to God. Especially the Church! I weep inside for this nation. I love this nation, even though it might not love me as well as I love it. As you know I served in the Armed Forces of this country, and I wore the uniform with pride. I am an American and I love this country and the flag. I love what it was supposed to stand for-One nation, under God, with liberty and justice for all. Has it left that, or have we ever really had that? America, you have left the principles that perhaps you were founded upon.

The Bible teaches that it is righteousness that exalts a nation. This is a time to mourn. This is a time to cry out to God, "Lord have mercy." This country has thrown away the Bible and thus has thrown away its victory. What will happen to our children? Who will teach them the true way? It is not easy for me to write this, but it is becoming progressively harder to be a Christian in America. The people of the land have given up righteousness for their rights. Let me ask you this. How can you have rights without righteousness? Where have we gone?

Before I go any further, I am reminded by the Holy Spirit how heavy it was on Jeremiah to give Judah a message from God concerning their downfall. How Judah, like her sister Israel, had turned away from God to serve foreign gods. God had dressed the nation of Israel in splendor and beauty. The Glory of God was upon her. However, they chose to serve other gods and brought destruction upon themselves in the Old Testament.

Listen, while the fall of a country can be sudden, the drifting away from God can be a slow and planned process. As the Word teaches us about our enemy-the devil-he is crafty, tricky, and can lead you away from God sometimes before you really see it. I believe it is time for America to check herself. If she doesn't, then she must brace herself. I don't know when all this will happen because He (God) did not tell me when. I can only tell you what He has shown me. As I write this book. I realized the persecution it could bring on my life, but I trust in the living God. Who likes to be the bearer of bad news I wonder? I don't. but this is the message that I believe God has given me to give to America.

In another dream that I have had, I believe I have seen something that pertains to the rapture. NO! I don't claim to know when. Jesus has made it very clear in the scriptures that time is not given t man. However, I believe it's time for the people of God to wake up and seek Him and His perfect will for their lives.

In this dream I heard the sound of a trumpet. When the trumpet blew the heavens raced away before me. There I saw a holy army as they were dancing before the Lord praising Him. They were shouting and waving banners of all sorts. As I watch all this, one of the soldiers brought his face near to me and said, "The time is not yet. The time is not yet." Now I must admit I don't know what all that means but I do know what I saw and the impact it has had on my life to get all things that I can right with God. Since I've become a Pastor, I've grown more in fear of the Almighty God.

Well, after about five years into my first marriage, I was sitting in church with my family waiting for service to begin and I asked her could she leave the church to obey God. Her reply to me made me feel like I had swallowed a brick. Her answer was no, she would never leave that church. At that very moment I knew I was in big, big trouble. I really didn't know what to do. So, I tried making myself content with not obeying God. I couldn't. No matter how determined I was to give up on the call, my heart ached for relief of the pain. I felt like I was dying on the inside.

Finally, one day she asked me, "Clint, can't you just be happy" And with tears running down my face I said, "I'm trying." I could see the end coming and was helpless to stop it. The very thing I thought I could keep, by trying to be happy was what I would eventually lose for being disobedient.

I was working with the State of North Carolina just before we separated. I got another job with a trucking company making a lot more money. After leaving the State I took my wife (my wife at that time) out to dinner to celebrate. At dinner I asked her after

11 years and 9 months of waiting, when would she be ready. She answered, she did not know.

After she answered my questions, I told her that God was closing this chapter in my life. I knew I had to answer the call and I knew it would cost me my marriage. As I said before, I don't blame her for anything. Looking back at my life, I now see how Satan all through my life had tried to stop God's plan.

Well, what I feared the most happened. One day I found myself alone with my nine-year-old son with me. Of our three children, the oldest had already left for the Navy and the baby girl went with my wife, and I kept the baby, my son. I tried to reconcile the marriage at the time that it happened by the wounds were too deep and the pain too great.

When it finally hit me that my marriage was over, I went into a state of depression. I thought my life was over. Of course, my family rallied around me to support me but only the Holy Spirit could heal the hurt within me. I began to feel guilty for what I had done. I couldn't understand how something like this could happen. We were a church family and Christians. All I wanted to do was obey God. Here we were a growing family, going to a good church, and thought whatever we faced we would come through. But it didn't work that way.

As I said I went into a state of depression and for days and days I cried. I now really understand what it means to be suicidal. I was so confused about what was happening. I can remember leaving home one evening, after the separation trying to find a friend of mine that lived just up the road from where I lived. I was so dazed by the blow of the enemy that I couldn't find it. So I turned around and drove back home. When I pulled in the drive and parked the car, I just sat there crying with the thoughts of suicide running through my mind. I had a very strange feeling come over me and I believe had I had a gun that day I might have hurt myself. But while sitting there, the Holy Spirit had me to look up at the house and I saw my little boy looking out the window for me. I remember the Lord dropping this statement in my spirit, "live for him".

I eventually had to leave the house where we lived because the pain was too great. I couldn't stand to look at the walls. So, my son and I moved in with my parents and lived there for about three months. Even so, I was still bleeding on the inside.

I had just move in with my parents when one night I went outside crying. I had lost my appetite and lost a lot of weight. I remember standing and looking up towards heaven and the Holy Spirit asked me could I pray for my wife and ask God to bless her. I said yes. Then he asked me could I pray and ask God to bless her and take her to her pinnacle of success even if it meant bringing someone else in her life to do it. Then I said no; I'm her husband; she's mine. Then the Holy Spirit spoke to me and said: "No. She is not yours; she is mine." He said to me "she is mine and you are mine".

In my prayer to God, I said I couldn't do that. He then asked me if I loved Him. I said yes. He then said, do it for me. So, I prayed the prayer He told me to pray. Not only did I pray that prayer that night, but also, I started praying it almost every day. Well from that point on I slowly began to heal and receive forgiveness from God and eventually I was ready to move back to my home. Things had not been resolved between my wife and me but I was now ready to face whatever I had to face with the Lord's help. I had not yet healed completely and would again have to deal with the memories that would bring tears again before complete healing would take place.

I know that God is a forgiving and loving Father. I have really learned that over the years as I walked (and continue to walk) with Him. He is truly a God of mercy. How can man not love and serve a God that loves the way He does. God is real and I know it.

As I said, I tried to reconcile the marriage even after I moved back into my own home. After having many conversations with her, I finally understood that I had to do what God had called me to do. I also realized I would have to retain a lawyer to finalize the divorce. One day, standing in front of my bathroom mirror, I cried a final cry. As I was standing there crying, the Holy Spirit told me to shut up.

Let me back up a minute. Knowing the divorce was coming, just before moving back into my own home, I had spoken with a lawyer. I knew him because we had gone to school together. Well, I went to see him about a divorce, but in order to see him I would have to deal with a woman that I didn't want to talk to at all. Let me tell you now, ironically this woman would later become my wife of today.

As I went from time to time to see my lawyer, I had to talk with a woman in his office that worked for him. Sometimes however, if the lawyer wasn't in I would just leave, avoiding conversation with her. When I first went there to seek advice, this lady tried to talk me into getting back with my wife. She would talk to me from time to time about praying to God about it. I told her I had been praying about it, however, my wife had said to me over the phone that she was going to be another man's wife. But what was strange to me is that this woman was telling everyone that came to see the lawyer about a divorce to pray first and ask God to reconcile the marriage. This little five-foot woman was doing God's will in the lawyer's office by turning away business. And the thing is, she did it boldly.

Well as time went on she finally told me that she would be getting the paperwork done. In other words, I would have to deal with her. At the time I didn't like it. But because she was working the case I had to talk to her.

One day while in her office, getting ready to leave, I heard a voice say there is your wife. I turned toward the entrance to see if my wife had walked in. the door was closed, and no one was standing thee so I turned back around and there was the five foot little woman looking at me with a smile. Well instantly, I rebuked that thought in the name of Jesus. I kept telling myself that had to be my flesh. I really didn't want to have anything to do with her then.

Well, closure finally came to me with the divorce of my first wife. But through the process of the divorce, however, I believed God was dealing with me. Every time I went to the lawyer's office, I would hear Him say take another look at her. We were not talking to each other about the case and just before I would leave the office I would turn and look at her when she wasn't looking. I did that for a while before I started accepting what I saw.

Well of course I knew I wasn't ready for another relationship, and she knew that too. But we became friends through my visits. I was really starting to enjoy her company at her workplace. As time went on and the divorce was over I still found myself going over thee. We finally agreed to start dating and did so for a year before I would ask her to marry me. I thank God for her! God used her to heal me and together we would start a brand-new life and ministry.

Listen, don't give up on God. He still has a plan for your life. You may have gone through a divorce and feel like God can't use you now. That's a lie. God will forgive you and heal you. It was a process for me but I'm now living in my Father's will. We are so excited about what God is doing in our lives. I don't care what kind of hurt you have experienced: IT'S NOT OVER..STAND UP AND REACH FOR YOUR DESTINY!

CHAPTER SEVEN

"IN HIS WILL"

I have often said, to get what is in the will, you have to get in His will. The Bible is God's written will. Jesus died to activate the will and rose again to see it through. I've met so many Christians that are believing God for so many things, but they're not doing what God has said in His written word in order for them to get it. It has been a long process for me and even though I have a long way to go; I'm finally in His will. The fight is not over for me, but I now have the victory.

As I said in the previous chapter, I married that five-foot little woman and God has blessed us to start our own ministry. We're fighting the good fight of faith and we're standing on the Word of God. I thank God for my gifted helpmeet. I'm learning to step back and let her operate in the many talents that God has give us to use in this ministry.

Listen men, the Bible teaches in Proverbs chapter 18:22 that who so finds a (true) wife finds a good thing and obtains favor from the Lord. I remember her telling me that the very day she saw me; she knew I had purpose in life, she knew God had called me.

However, after getting married things didn't just turn around like that. I have a lot of respect for my wife because of what she went through with me. The marriage started off fine, but when we started a Bible study that later became a ministry, I got the shock of my life. I started learning things about me. I started learning about things that I had not yet been completely freed of. I found out how insecure I really was. I look back at all of this now and I see just how much strength my wife had to have for the both of us. I did not realize just how much damage the divorce had left in my life.

The divorce had dazed me and even though I knew God had called me, I was afraid of getting hurt and found it really hard to trust God. That's where my wife, Rosa stepped in. She watched me step forward and then step backwards again and again with my confidence in God. What I now realize is that God had given me a giant in a five-foot woman.

God has used Rosa to heal me, stand me up, and push me forward. Because of my emotional insecurities I almost shattered my wife (Rosa) emotionally and ruined my marriage. The very gift that God had given me to pray and work with and to bring me out of a shattered world, I was now shutting out because of pain.

I failed to mention that during the courtship to this wonderful woman, whom I married, my mother was diagnosed with cancer. We were married on her birthday, and she was present at the wedding. My mother died 34 or 35 days later. Through it all God is a wonderful Father. He truly is an awesome God.

As I said, because of the pain I had inside I really hurt my wife in the beginning of our marriage. She kept trying to get me to admit that I did not trust her, but I wouldn't. She wasn't trying to have something to beat me over the head with, she wanted me to face the truth. You see, what you don't face, you will never overcome.

There are so many things in our lives and relationships that we don't want to face. The devil uses this to block our freedom in God and our blessings from God. The very things that I would not confess because of pride, the enemy was using to destroy. Many times, we don't know who we are until a test comes. However, when you are in a test and when you face opposition, it can be a place of discovery in your life. Whatever is not tested in your life is not known, and knowledge brings freedom and growth.

> *Study and be ager and do your utmost to present yourself to God approved (tested by trial), a workman who has no cause to be ashamed, correctly analyzing and accurately dividing (rightly handling and skillful teaching) the word of truth.* 2 Timothy 2:15

Let's look at tested by trial. I was being tested by this (and other trials) trial and wasn't passing the test because of pride. When I finally started to confess my sin of distrust of my mate, I became free. As God continued to use my wife to prop me up in my purpose, I began to see her gifts and some of her purpose. She is truly a helpmate. She doesn't compete with me; she completes me. The devil tried to blind my eyes and use me to stop God's purpose for our lives.

I was a very insecure person when it came down to my wife. One way in which it manifested itself in our lives was as distrust. The devil tried to make me think that my wife was unfaithful. When we got into conversations about people being unfaithful, I would always try to make clear if she was unfaithful to me, she would have to go and never come back. Well, one day we were talking about this, and she finally told me, "Clint it is you who is afraid of being unfaithful." Of course, I had a rebuttal. My reply was, "I've never been unfaithful." Listen, your past can come up again to hinder your future. Growing up seeing and hearing how women could not be trusted made it hard for me to trust Rosa. My divorce played its part.

Now I know what you're thinking. Just maybe it was distrust that caused the divorce. Not so. Before the divorce, I had grown to trust the woman I was married to first. The devil was trying to frustrate what God was working in my life when I finally got in His will. The only way he could again hinder or even stop God's plan was to get me out of God's will. So, he tried to make me think that my wife (Rosa) was unfaithful. But little did I know that I would be the one tested. I hurt my wife badly when she realized that I didn't think she was faithful. In fact, one night after having a heated conversation she said to me, "You think I'm a whore", and then turned her back to me in the bed and cried all night. I knew I had grieved the Holy Spirit and it would be a long time before she would actually heal from that.

As I said, I would be the one tested in my faithfulness. I actually thought I had gotten past all that. But what I have learned is never let your guard down. Never assume you cannot fall or think you can hide sin.

In all of this, I became attracted to a young lady. Something that I thought could not happen. She too was attracted to me. I began to sense the pull and the temptation became stronger and stronger. I tried not to let it show but what I thought was not seen was being seen the entire time. I later realized when this thing was brought to light my wife already knew.

It became a big problem in our marriage and while the threat was not seen in the ministry it was there. Satan wanted to destroy our marriage and our ministry. There were moments when I couldn't get this young lady out of my head. It was a trick of the enemy and the young lady was totally blind to the work of the devil. She really didn't know what the enemy was after. I do know what it means to have praying people around you. Sometimes the temptation was overwhelming, and I really thought at one point I may fall. I fasted and prayed and got counseling from other pastors older than I, but it still seemed at one time I was going to give in to it. I have to admit that at one point my flesh was crying out for it. There was a real battle going on. I realized that two things were going on. One, I had become relaxed, and I let the enemy in. Two, this was a test and it revealed to me the places in my life that needed fortification. I realized that if there are any weak places in your home relationship the devil will make it his business to find them.

As I said, this young lady was also attracted to me. This may have happened as we dealt with each other. It's never wise to deal with the opposite sex, one on one. I knew that and still fell into the trap. But what the devil meant for bad, God turned it around for the good. I had to be honest with my wife. The Bible teaches that we have to confess our sin. However, when I told her, she let me know that she already knew.

Before I go any further, here are some questions I asked my wife about the experience.

1) Clint – How could you tell I was attracted to this young lady?
Rosa – By the attention you gave her. How you talked to her. How you looked at her. By the things you said to her.
2) Clint – When did you realize that I was attracted to her, what were your first thoughts?

> Rosa – Betrayed. I blamed myself. What did I do to turn him to someone else? I as too trusting. I felt anger.
> 3) Clint – Caught between me (your husband) and the young lady that I was attracted to, and you loved, what helped you to stand?
> Rosa – My relationship with God.
> 4) Clint – What is it that you can share with others to help them avoid this type of attack
> Rosa – I really don't know if it is avoidable. I realize that we are all humans, and we can make a mistake. Never think that it can't happen to you. and never say what you won't do. (End of questions).

Understand this, no matter how hard you may try to hide what is going on inside of you, many times you only make it all the more obvious. There might be times when it was not readily seen but the Bible teaches us that your sins will find you out.

In the book of Numbers chapter 32 and verse 23 it teaches that your sins will find you out. So, there is nothing done in secret that will stay a secret. It will come to light. It will be uncovered.

But this episode in my life was nothing but the enemy. I thank God for the relationship I have with Him and my wife. Because of it, when I was under that kind of attack I was able to share it with my wife. I realized that this was not the only time the devil was going to try me with that. However, what it has done for me is made me realize that no matter how long you've been saved, you can't stand without Jesus Christ being the head of your life.

Let me take this time to remind you that, this chapter is about being in God's will. I was a truck driver for a well-known trucking company. And as you have read in this book I've had several other jobs but God's plan still came to pass.

So what are some things that I can share with you about what to do when you know God has a specific call on your life? I say specific because we all are called to do something. For example, we all have been called to repentance. All of mankind have been called to turn to God for forgiveness of sin. There are those of course that God have placed a specific call upon, such as Pastors, Prophets, Evangelist Apostles, and Teachers.

> *Because of this brethren, be all the more solicitous and eager to make sure (to ratify, to strengthen, to make steadfast) your calling and election; for if you do this, you will never stumble or fall.* 2 Peter 1:10

First let me say, be diligent in making certain God's calling and choosing of you. Understand that you will be tested and purged. However, I believe there are some in the Body of Christ that either doesn't realize this fact or they don't recognize when they are being tested and purged. Be careful not to refuse God's way in which He has chosen to make you.

Secondly, ask God to place you in a ministry that can mentor and mature you. After asking God to lead you, allow Him to do so. Sometimes you won't like where He wants you to go or what He wants you to do. Too often we expect the things that God has promised to do to happen overnight. And that is not always the case. Because we get in a hurry, God will not get in one. Become an effective part of the ministry God places you under. Become faithful to God where He places you to serve. Do not become judgmental and condemning of the leadership that you are under. Don't become self-righteous; it will poison your effectiveness.

Take hold of the vision of the leaders and help bring their vision to pass. Supporting another vision will help birth your vision. Always keep a teachable spirit. Remember, to walk with God you must learn to sacrifice. Jesus sacrificed and you will to.

Listen, what God has promised He will do. I'm sure of it. For many years I waited and went through much, but God delivered me out of them all. Allow God to heal every part of you by opening up to Him in honesty. He will bring wholeness and purpose to your life. be obedient to His every word.

And I am convinced and sure of this very thing, that He who began a good work in you will continue until the day of Jesus Christ (right

> *up to the time of His return), developing (that good work) and perfecting and bringing it to full completion in you. Phil. 1:6*

So beloved, now is the time to stand. Stand in the midst of battle with your faith in God. Hold fast to your confession of faith. Allow the Holy Spirit to burn all things of the flesh from you. I understand process. You may have a call of God on your life. Only you and God really know but remember this. Even though you have a call on your life, you still must be made into the vessel God desires for you to be. Only God can do it. Man can promote you, but only God can anoint you to do the work in which you were called. Don't give up on God because God won't give up on you. Seek His face, run after His heart, and He will reveal His will to you.

My wife and I face many challenges. But we face them with our hope in Jesus Christ. When I stopped working to establish a ministry in a small town, I knew then what God had called me to but I still had to be tried. Our income was cut in half but God has proven Himself over and over again to us. I truly know what it means to have a virtuous woman.

> *A capable, intelligent, and virtuous woman – who is he who can find her? She is far more precious than jewels and her value is far above rubies or pearls. The heart of her husband trusts in her confidently and relies on and believes*

> *in her securely, so that he has no lack of honest (gain) or need of (dishonest) spoil. She comforts, encourages, and does him only good as long as there is life within her.* Proverbs 31:10-12

These verses of scripture fit my wife. I could write this last chapter completely about her. She has brought only good in my life, and she has paid just as great a price as I have. Many of the successes that I have experienced in my life have come through her by the hand of God. She is truly about my success. Everything she does, she does for the success of her husband. She is a very smart woman, and I will forever praise God for bringing her into my life. She has gone through many hurts that I caused, and she still has stood by me and fought for my cause. Who can find a virtuous woman of this sort? It takes a Godly woman to go through what my wife has gone through and still stand by her husband. The devil has attacked me many times, and my wife, bleeding herself, have stood firmly in her place by my side and fought with me.

My wife has worked hard in this ministry and in our home. She has never once that I recall stood up and said what she has done. She consistently pushes me to the front and encourages me to stand. What I have come to realize is that other than Jesus, she is far more precious to me than anything. How could I ever repay a woman like this? What could I give in thanks for her faith and strength? What could I give her to match what she has been for me? I have asked my wife many times to forgive me, and I ask her again in this book to forgive me so the whole world can hear it. She is truly a virtuous woman, wife and friend. Rosa I thank God for you.

Well, when I look back at my life it has been a long journey to get here. But because of God, I made it. Because of God, my wife and I will fight the good fight of faith and through Jesus Christ accomplish all that has been sat before us.

Let this book be a testimony of what God can do for you and through you if you will stand and keep the faith. I have not been perfect, but I've been forgiven. I now live for Jesus Christ. I write this book to tell those who have given up to stand up and trust God. You've been forgiven by the grace of God. Now, let the weak say that they are strong. I'm not telling you that everything will change overnight. But I am saying that no matter what has beset you, get up and glorify God. Receive forgiveness from God and live your life in Jesus Christ to the fullest. Know that opposition is a place of discovery. A place to find out just how wonderful God is and just how much He really loves you.

Yes, I know you've been hurt. I'm sure you might say that you are tired. It's time to let the Lord be your strength and let the Lord fight your battles. Hold your head up and be strong, for greater is He that is in you than he that is in the world.

Remember that the enemy (Satan) is a created being and not God. Satan has limitations. Knowing the persecution that might come from writing this book, I still step forward for Jesus Christ. I don't know what tomorrow might bring, but I know I can face tomorrow with faith in Jesus Christ. I can't explain why things happened the way they did in my life, but I can take my life and now glorify God. He is truly my strength and my redeemer. He brought me through, and He can bring you through if you allow Him to. Make the choice to stand today and don't give up. I said stand up! But stand up in Jesus Christ and Jesus Christ will stand with you. VICTORY is waiting for you. Don't wait any longer, stand now and claim your place of victory. Do it today!

If you read and find yourself, I encourage you to stand and let my wife and I, and Upon This Rock Ministries stand with you. God loves you and so do we. Victory, Victory, Victory! With Jesus it all spells Victory!

God Bless You
Clint and Rosa Burwell

www.ingramcontent.com/pod-product-compliance
Lightning Source LLC
LaVergne TN
LVHW011718060526
838200LV00051B/2947